I0505267

AI TAOISM
COLORING BOOK

Hey there, I'm Jeremy Hubert Burt. I was feeling inspired and decided to use a prompt to create some 3D coloring book pages. The prompt I used was:

"Design a captivating coloring book page featuring the profound symbol of Taoism. Against a pristine white background, use bold black lines to illustrate the intricate details of the symbol, evoking a sense of harmony and contemplation.

Create elegant and serene background designs that complement the Taoism symbol, immersing the viewer in a world of wisdom and tranquility. These designs should inspire introspection and a connection to nature.

Incorporate various shapes such as flowing curves, gentle waves, and symbolic elements throughout the page, inviting individuals to explore the depths of Taoist philosophy. Add serene phrases in a font that captures the essence of balance and serenity, enhancing the sense of tranquility and discovery.

Outline the symbol with bold black lines, clearly defining the boundaries for coloring. This empowers enthusiasts to infuse the symbol with their own interpretations and artistic expression, using the striking contrast of black and white.

The coloring book page promises a journey of contemplation and enlightenment into the realm of Taoist symbolism. It invites individuals to engage in the art of coloring, providing a delightful sense of relaxation and stress relief. Embrace the profound power of the Taoism symbol amidst the timeless contrast of black and white."

After creating the design, I decided to edit the levels in GIMP in greyscale image mode to give it that extra touch of depth and detail. The whole process only took me a day, and I'm really happy with the results.

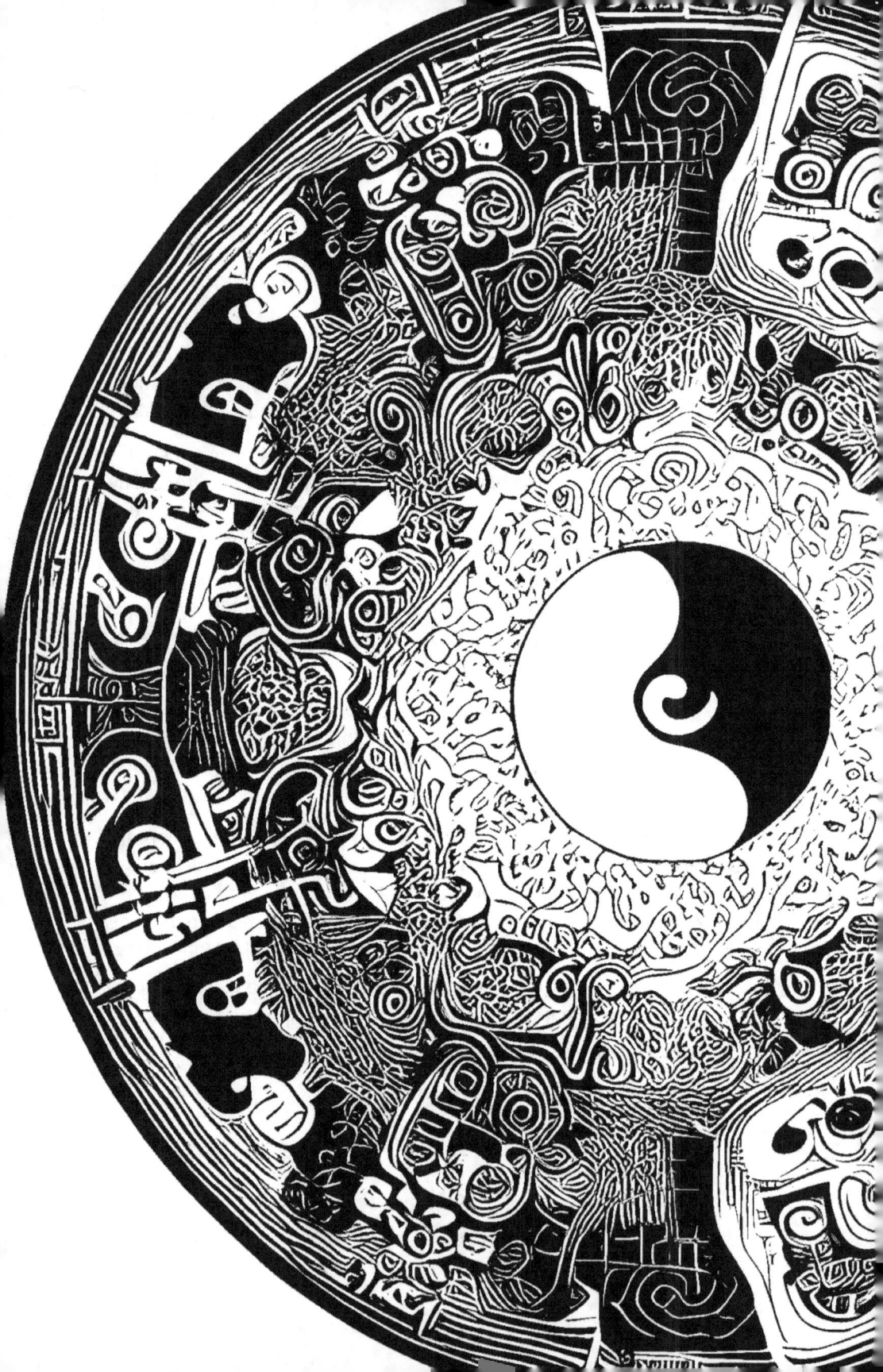

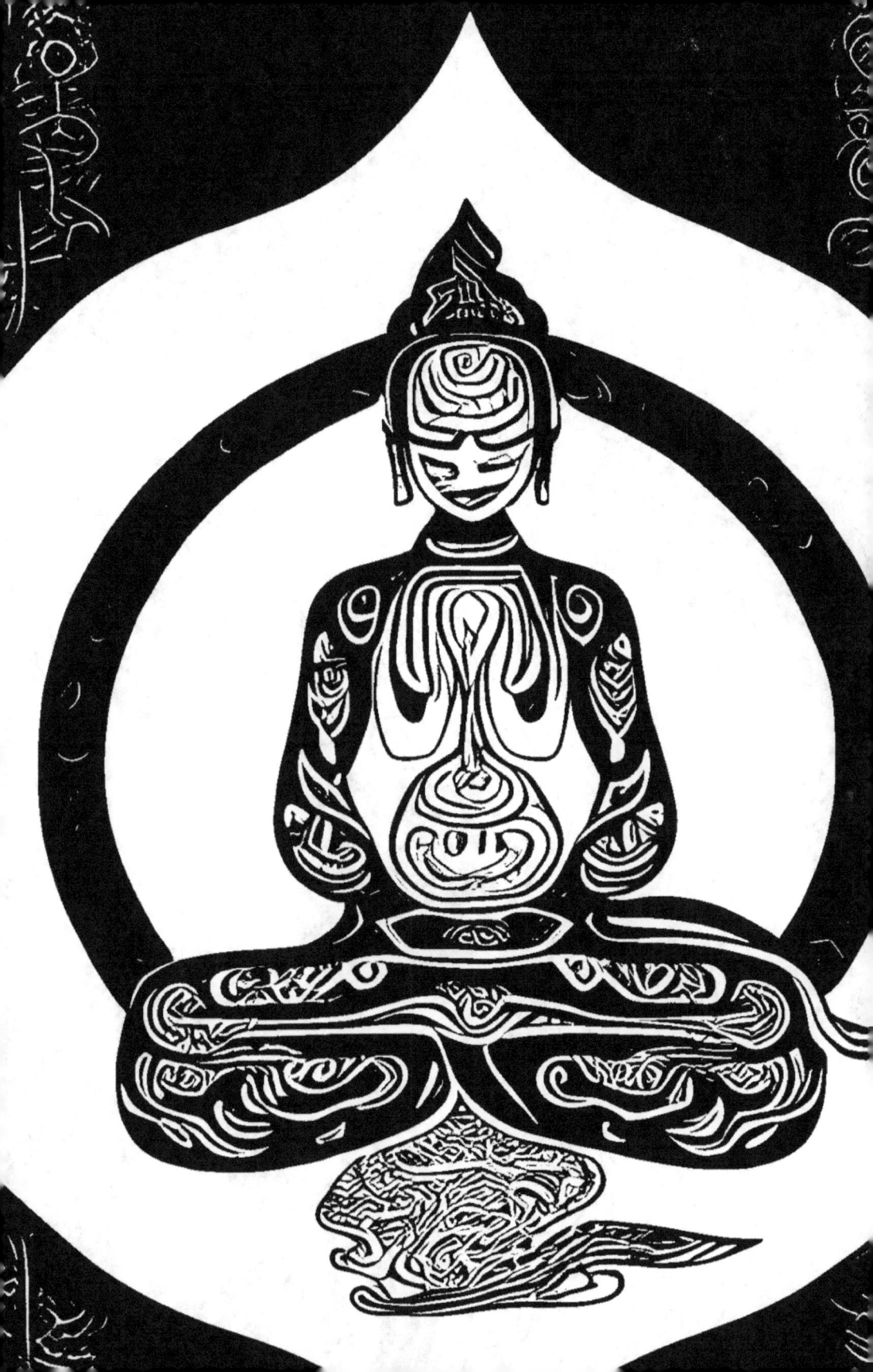

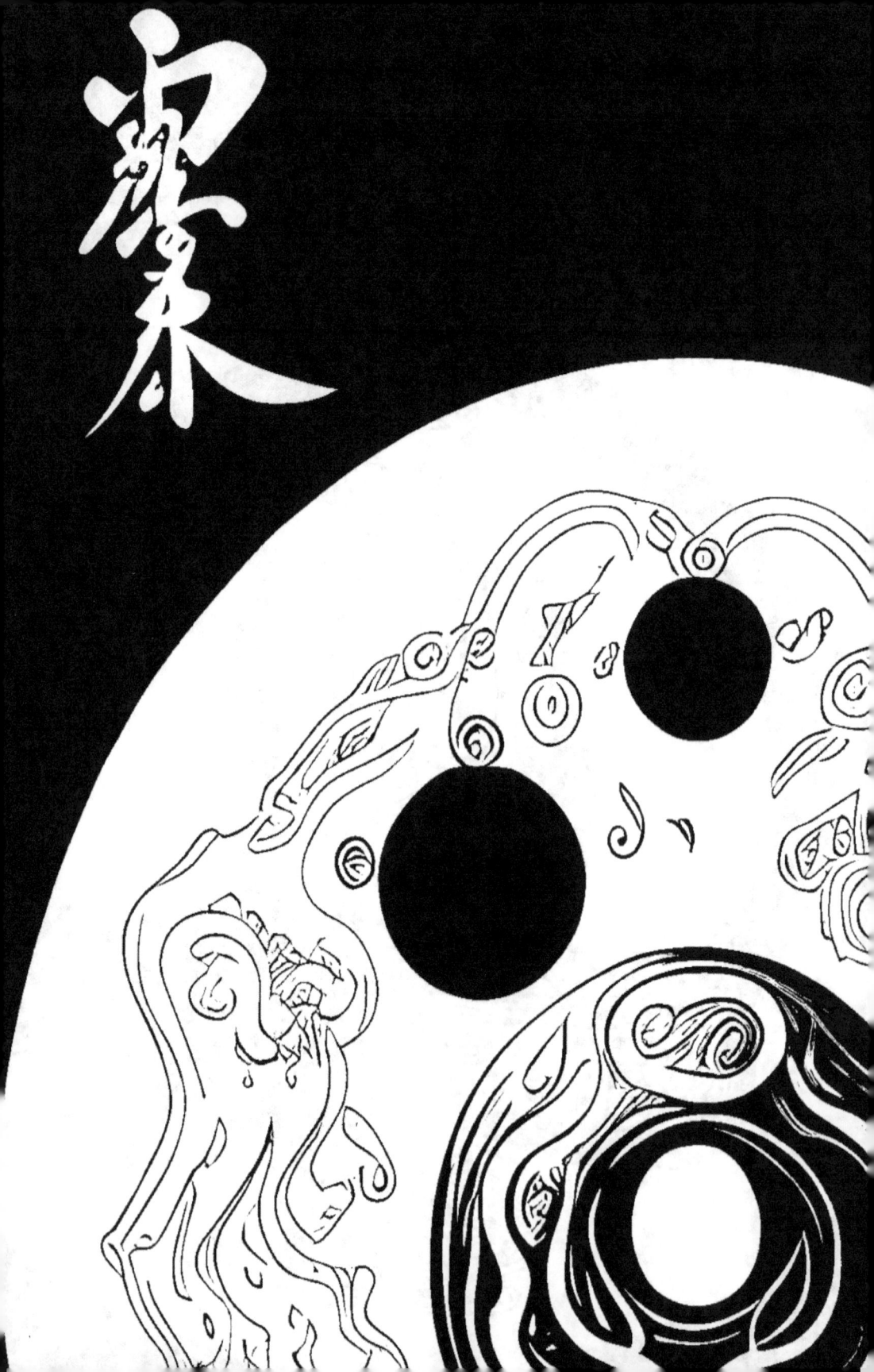

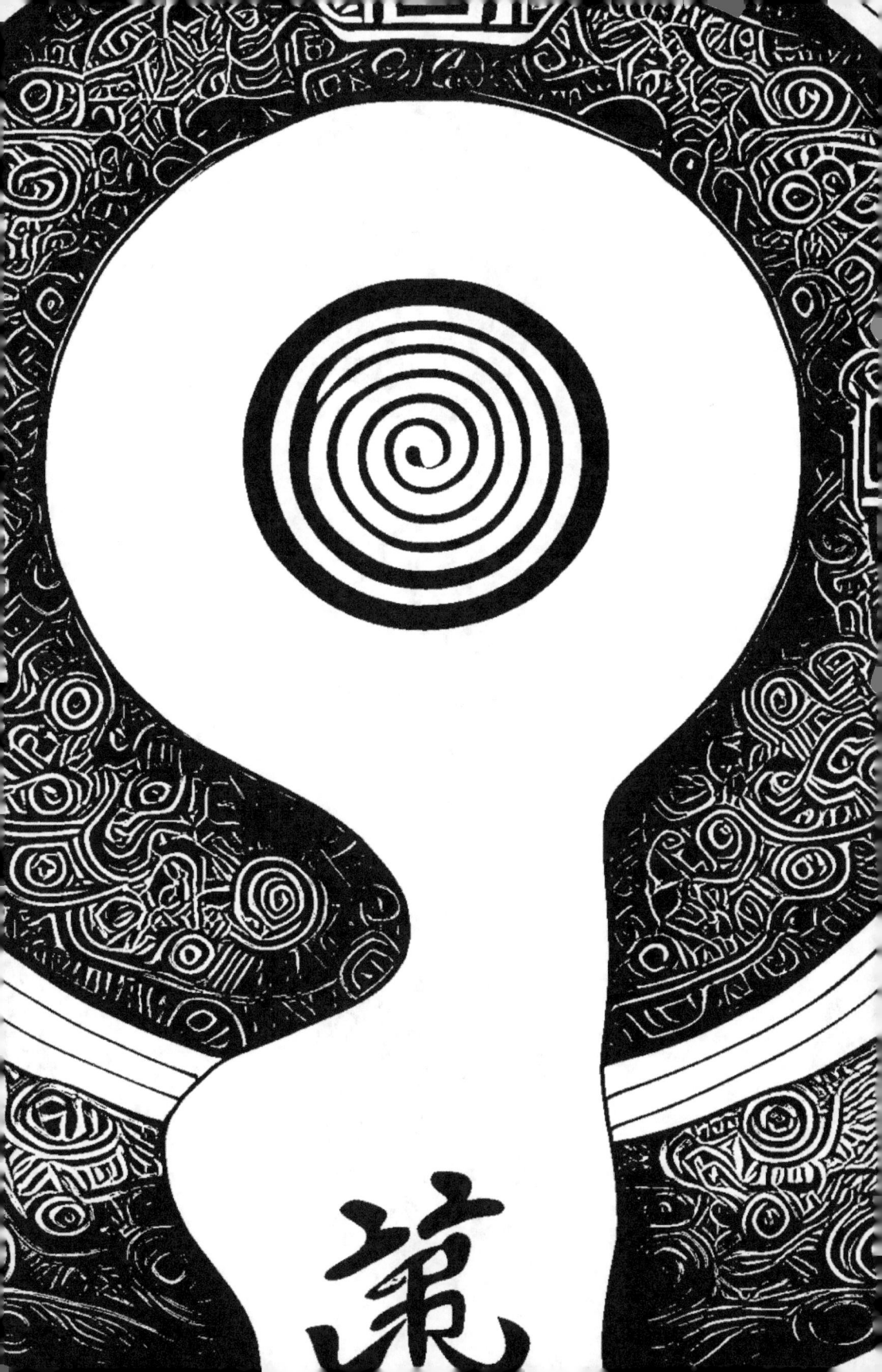

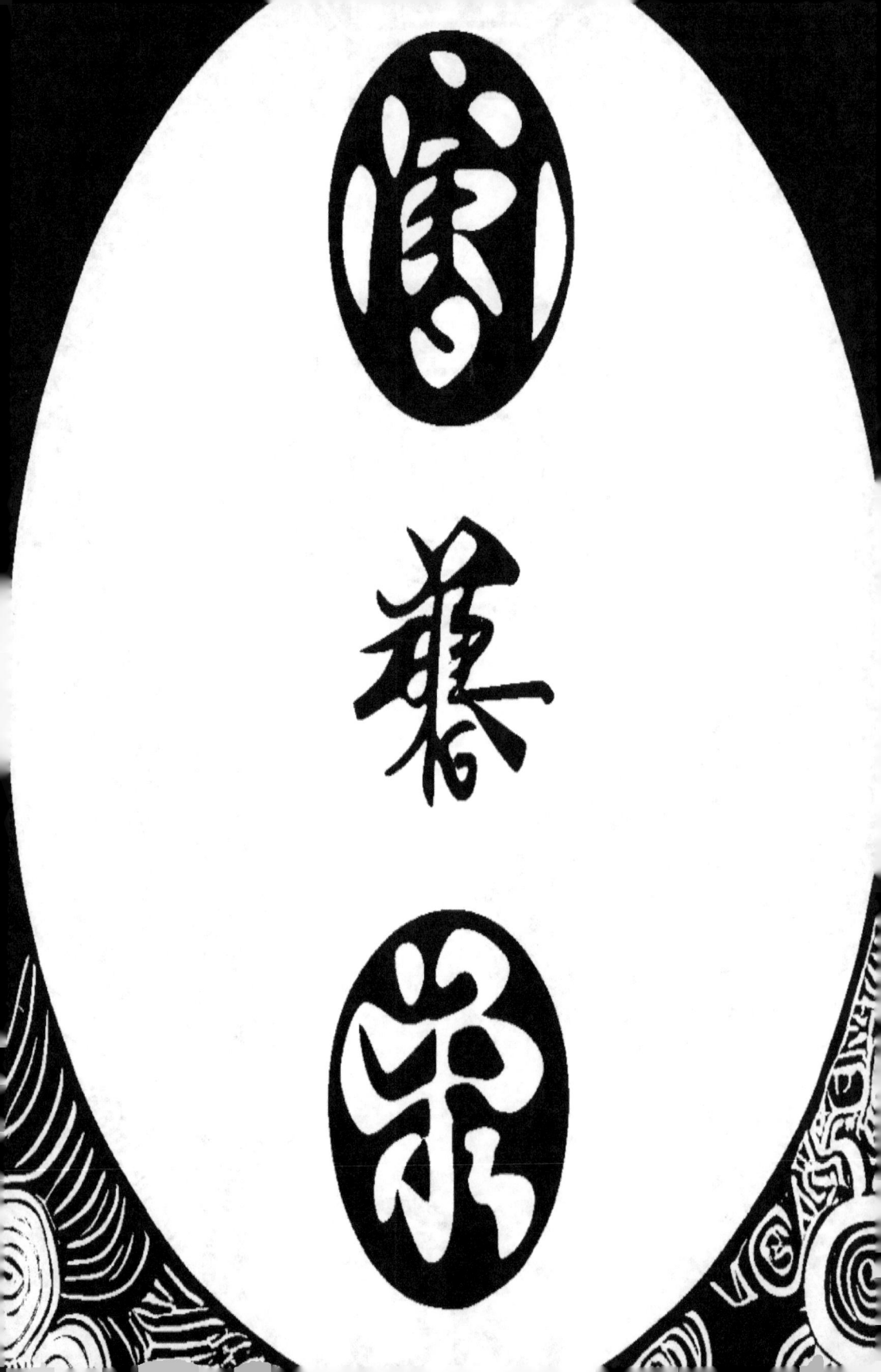

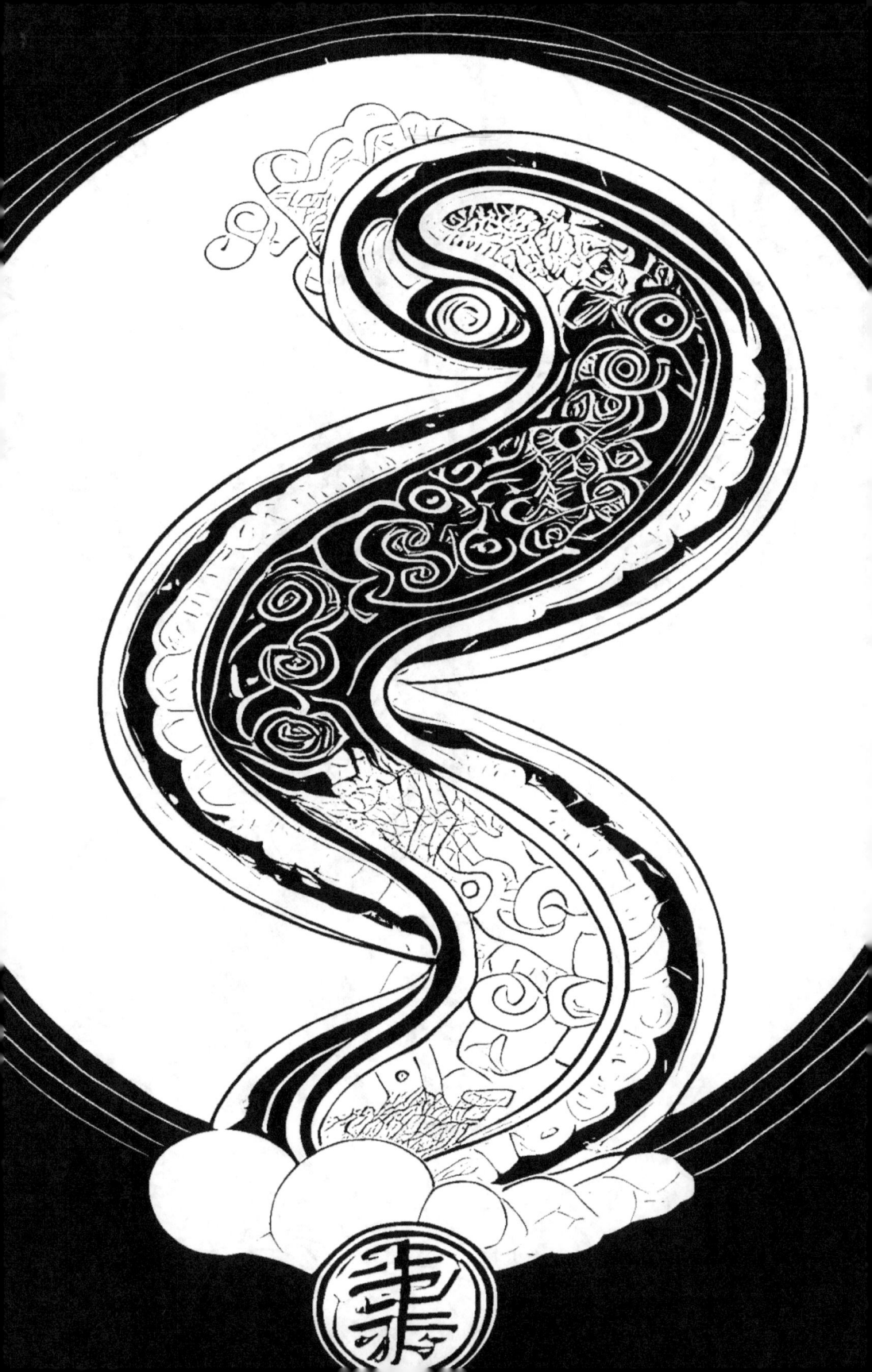

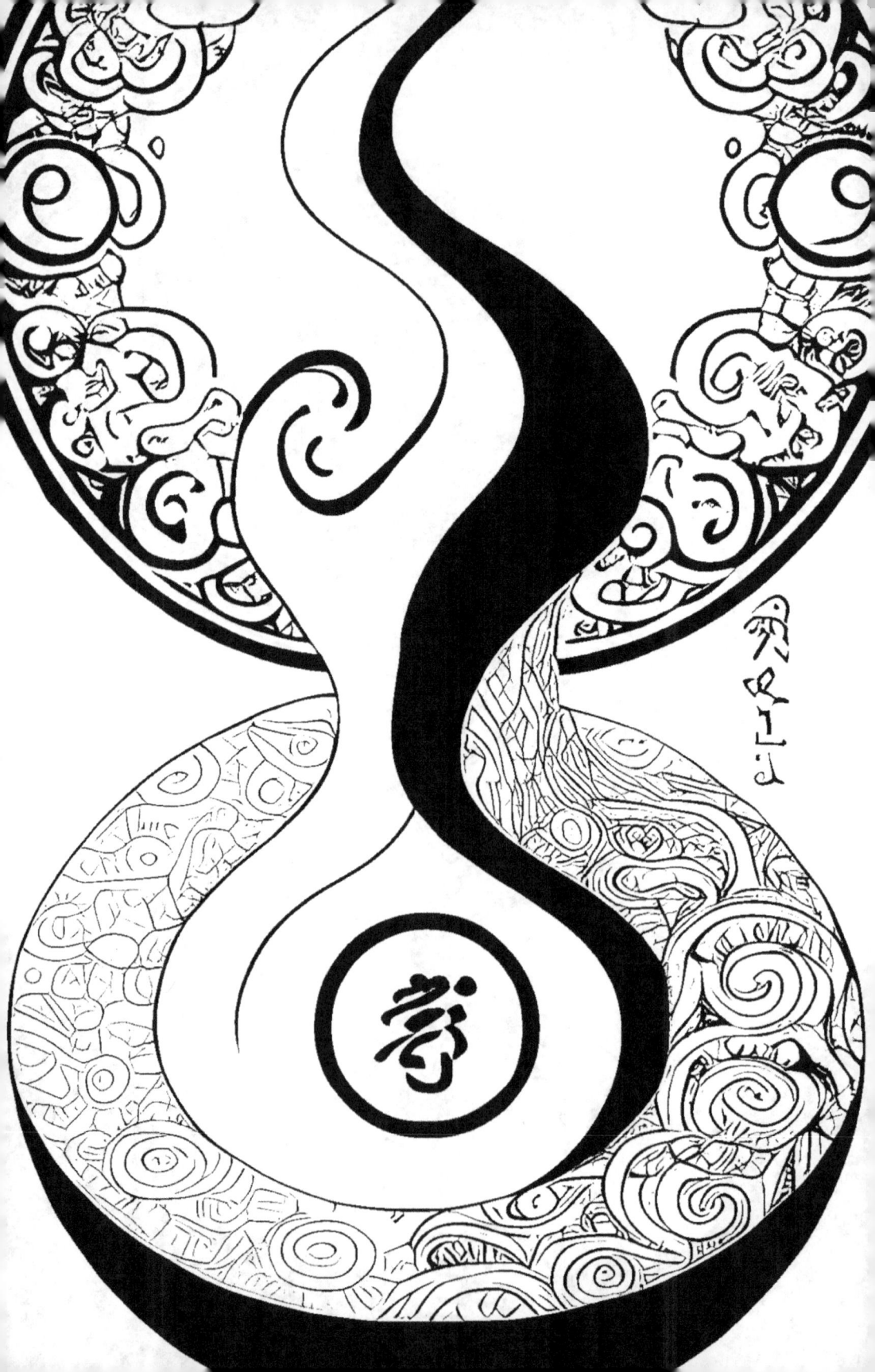

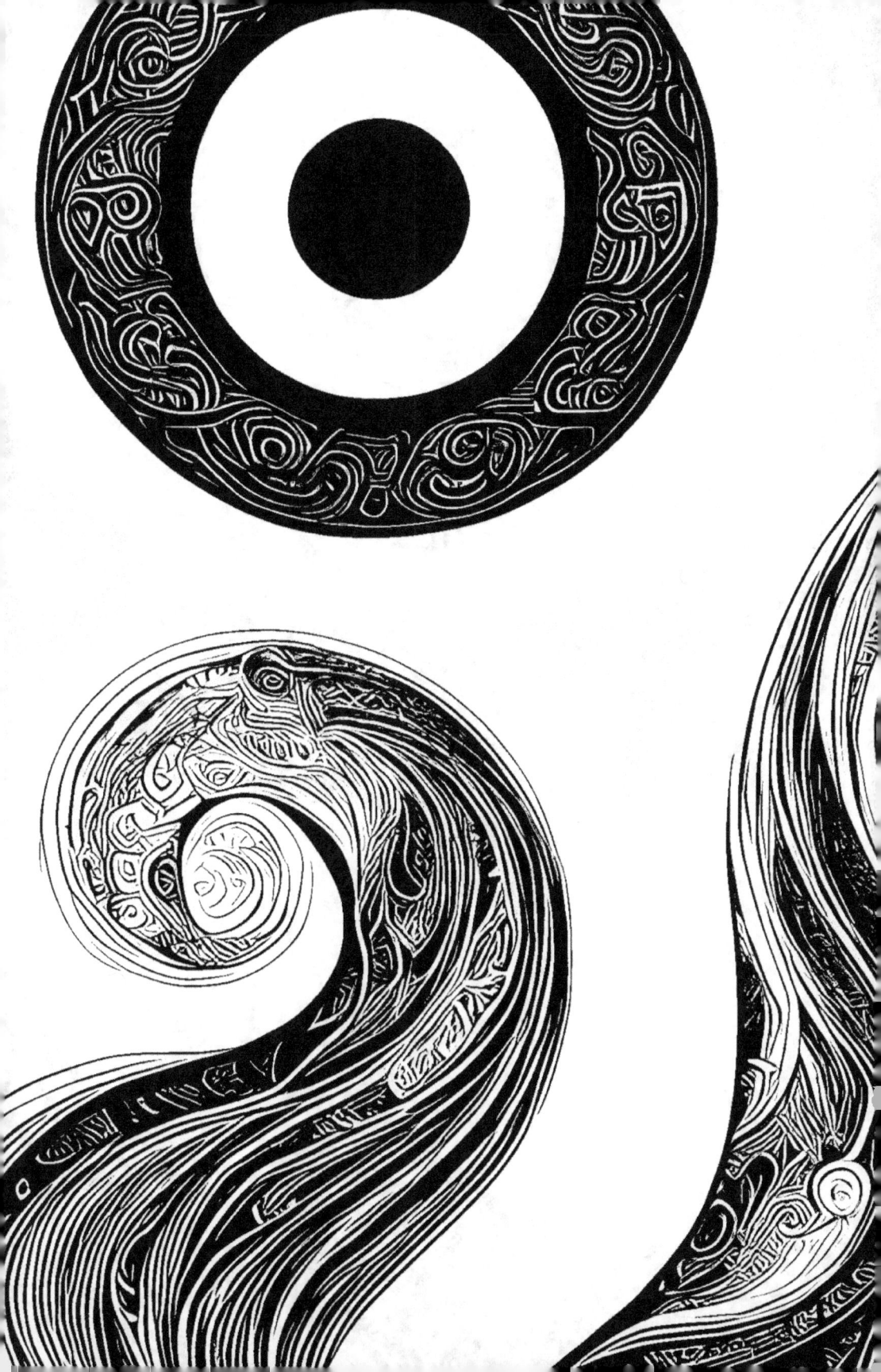

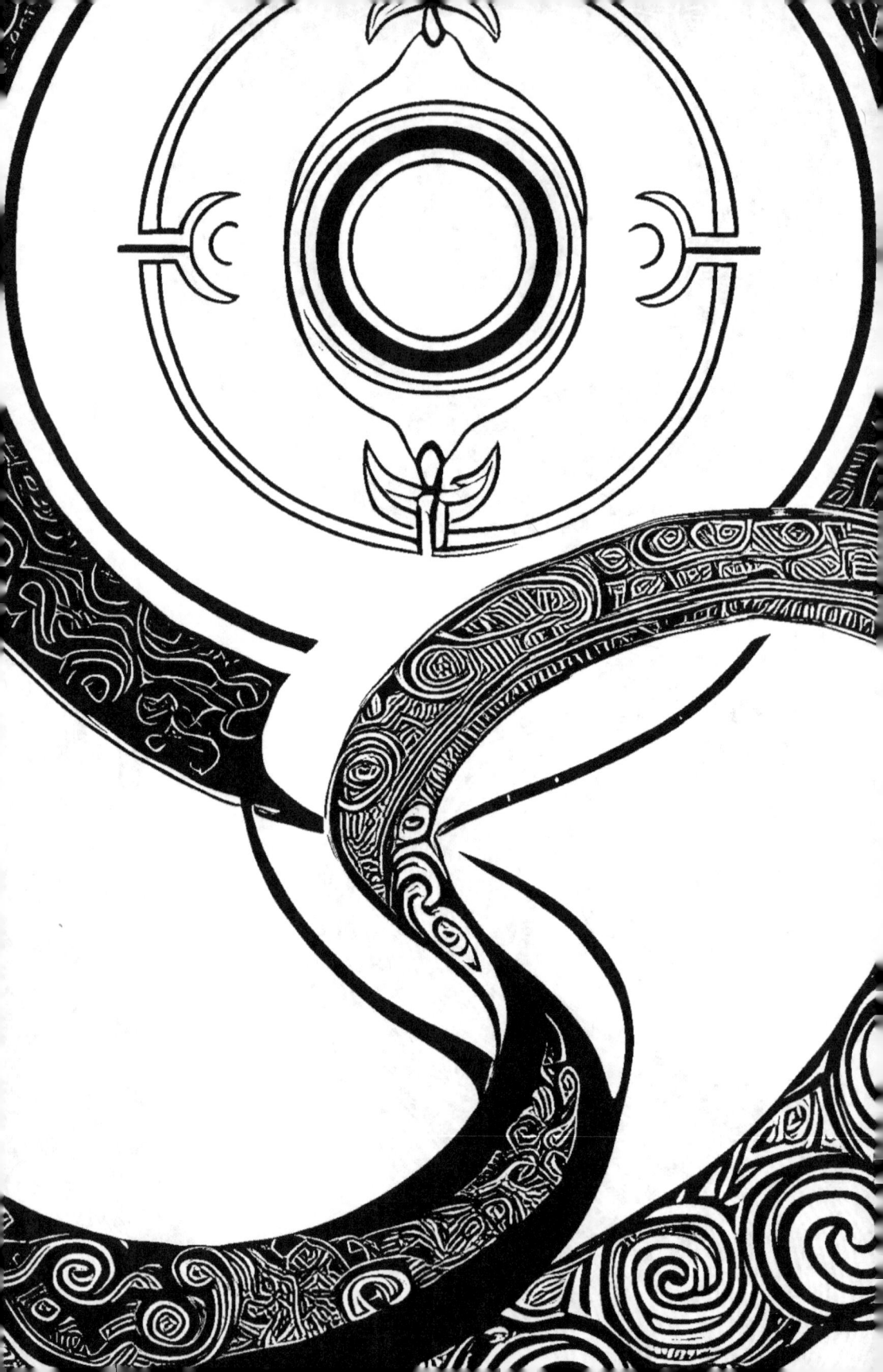

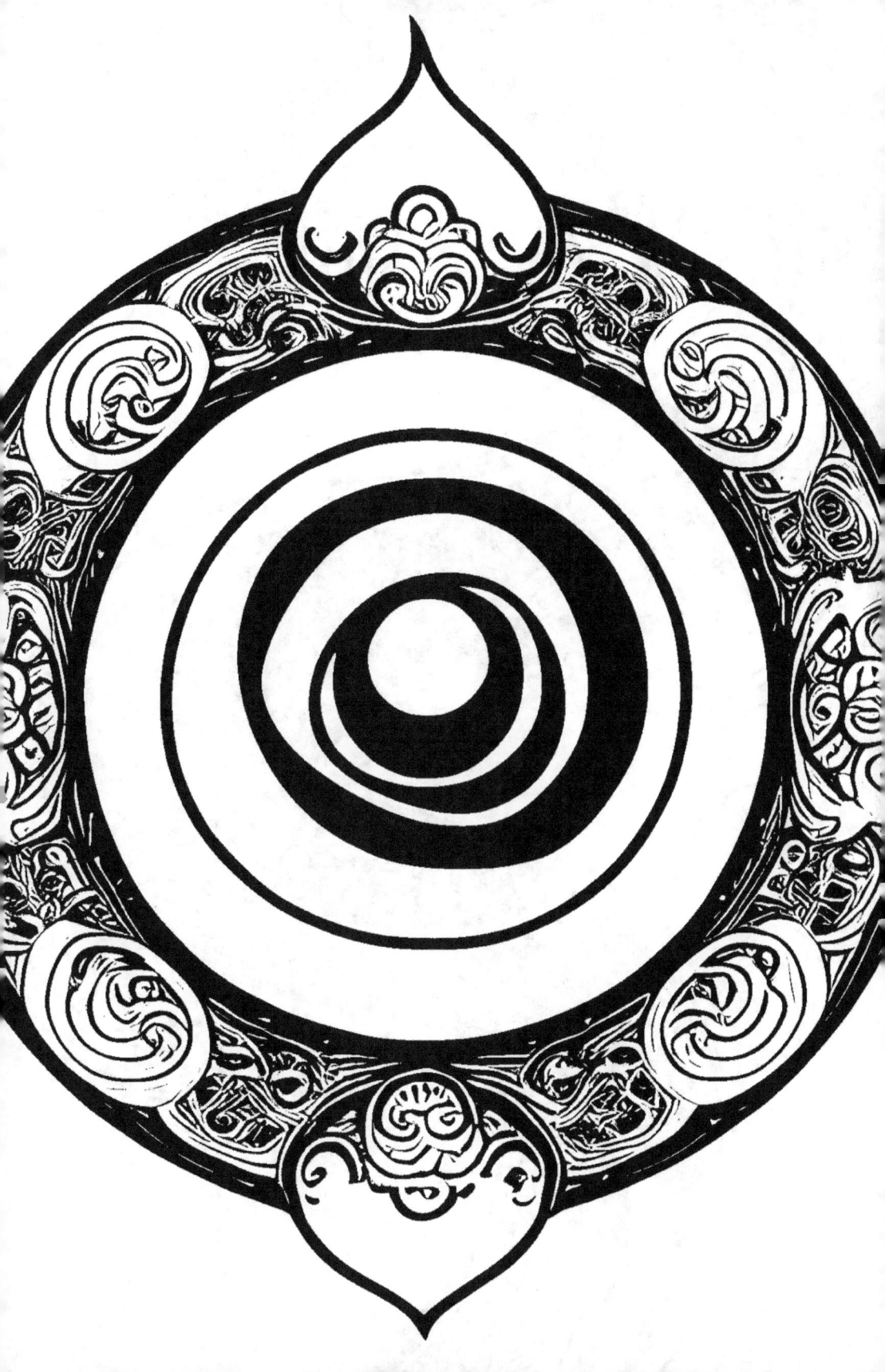

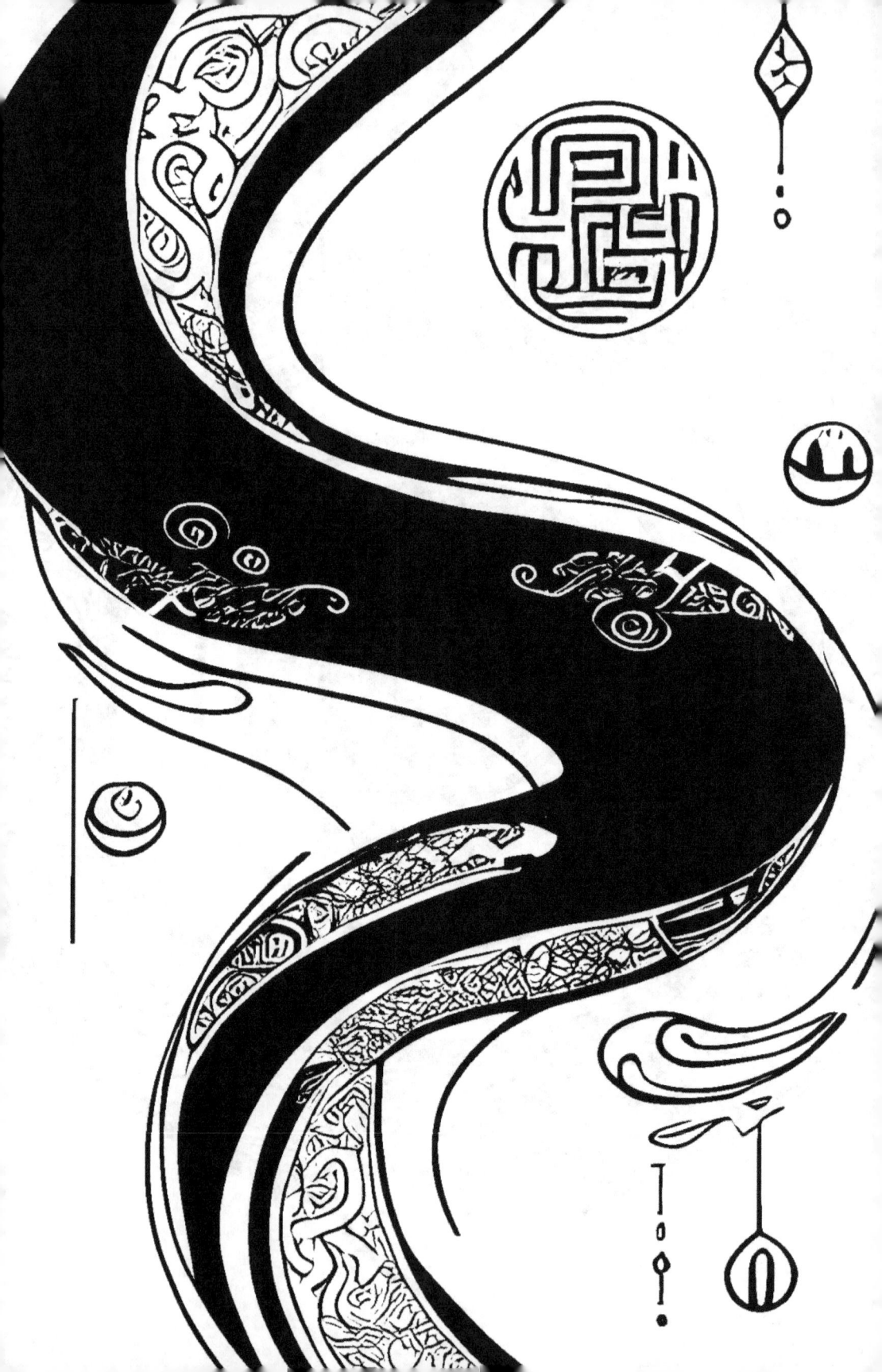

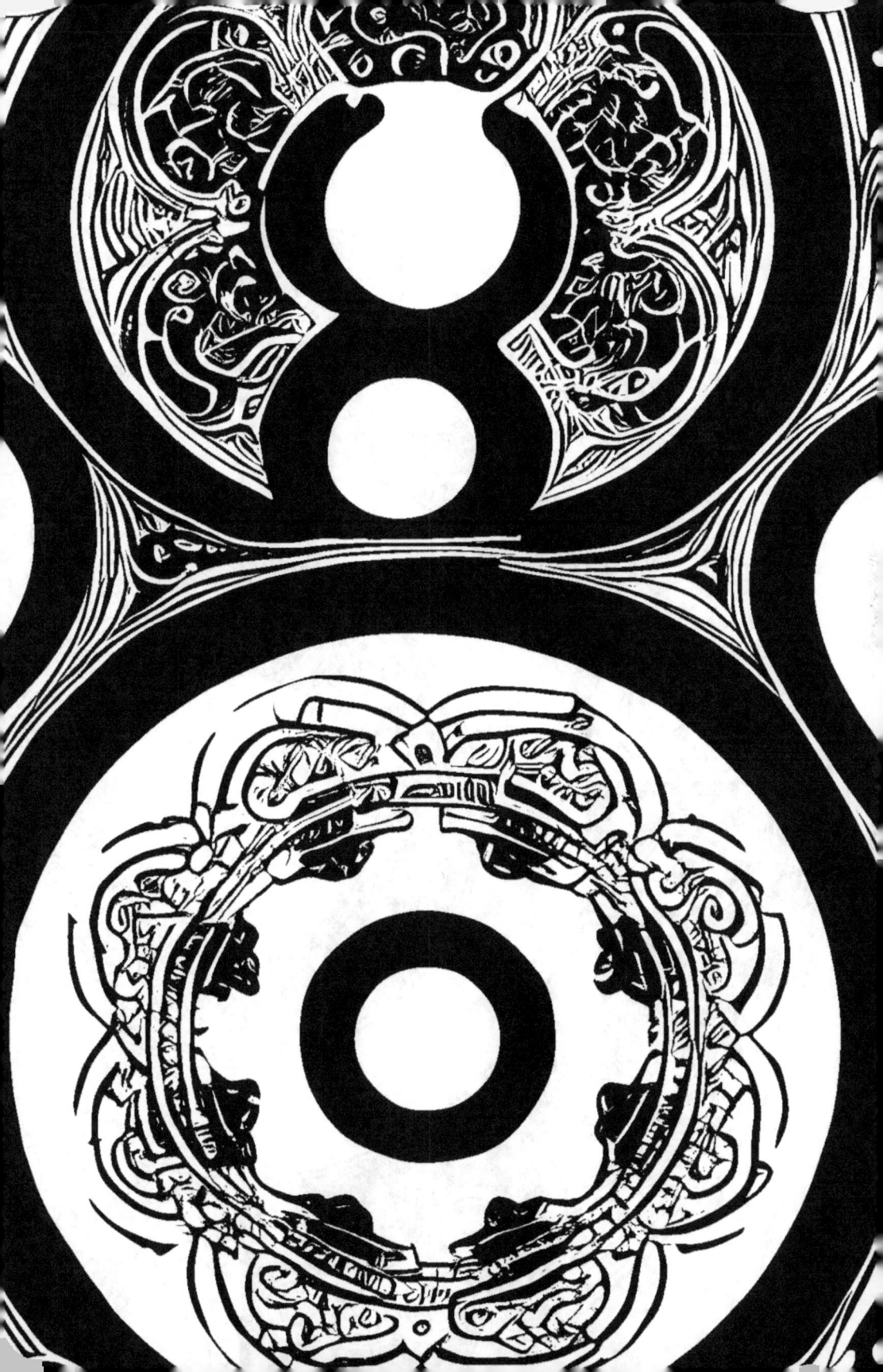

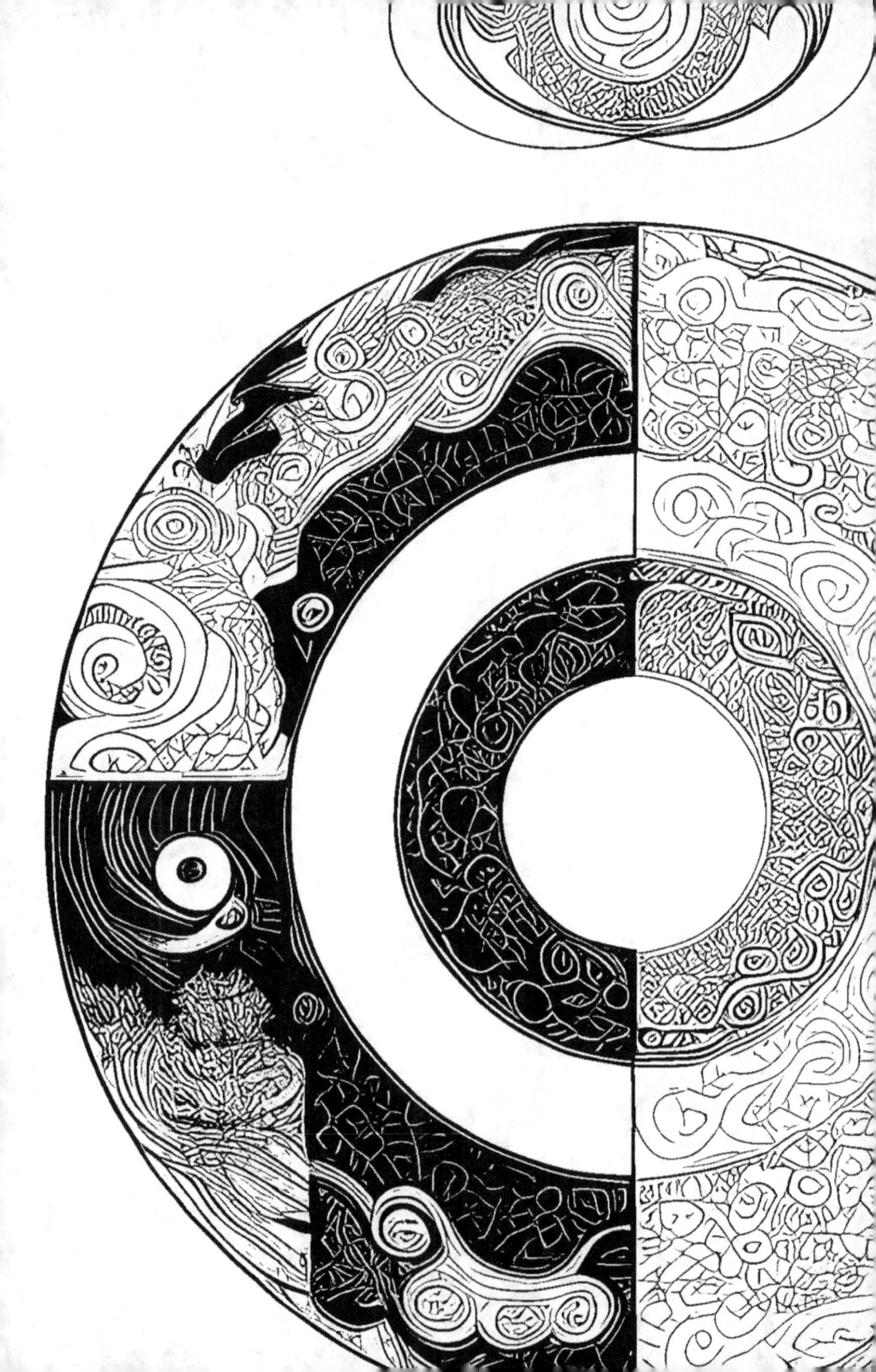

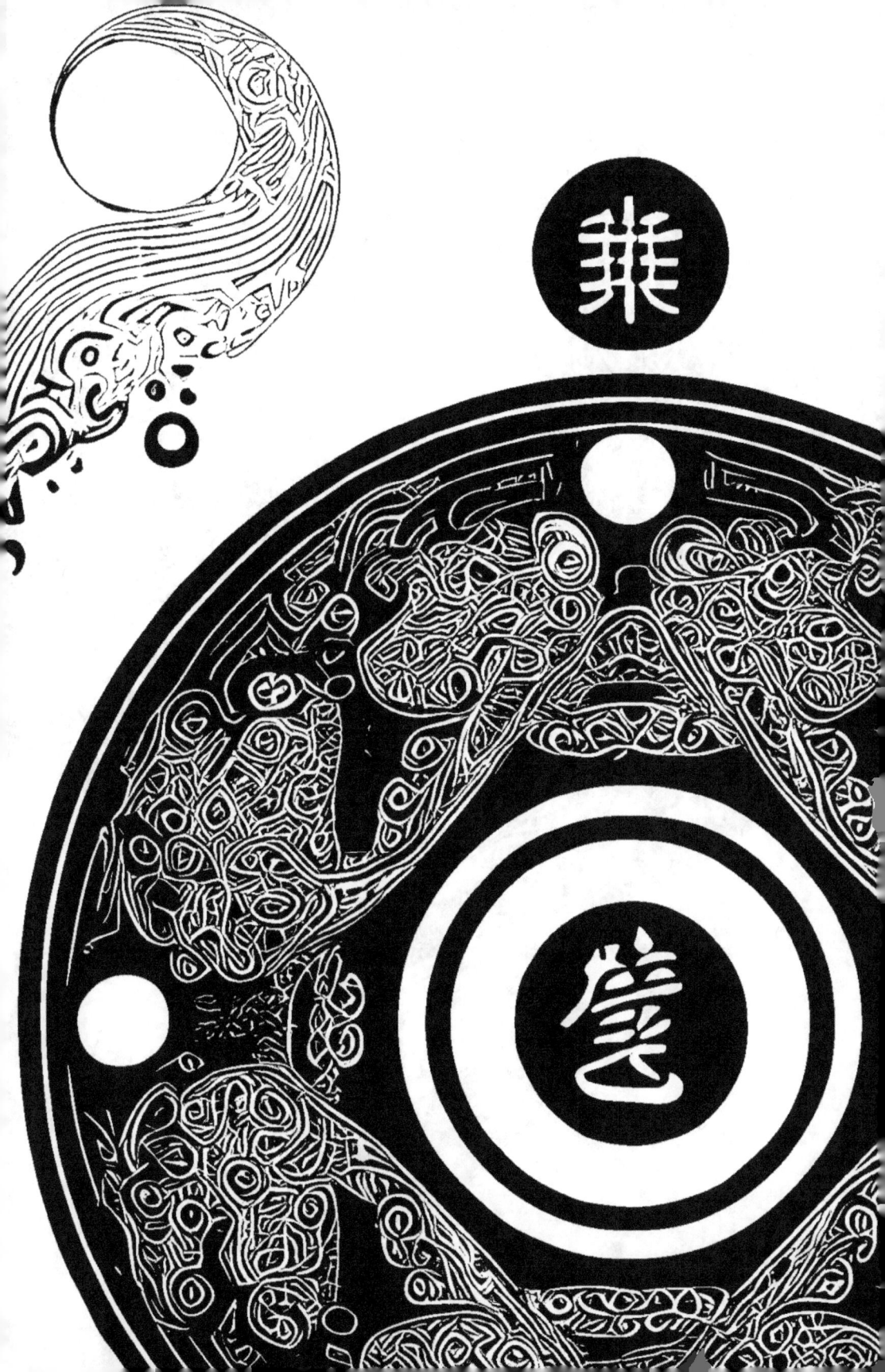

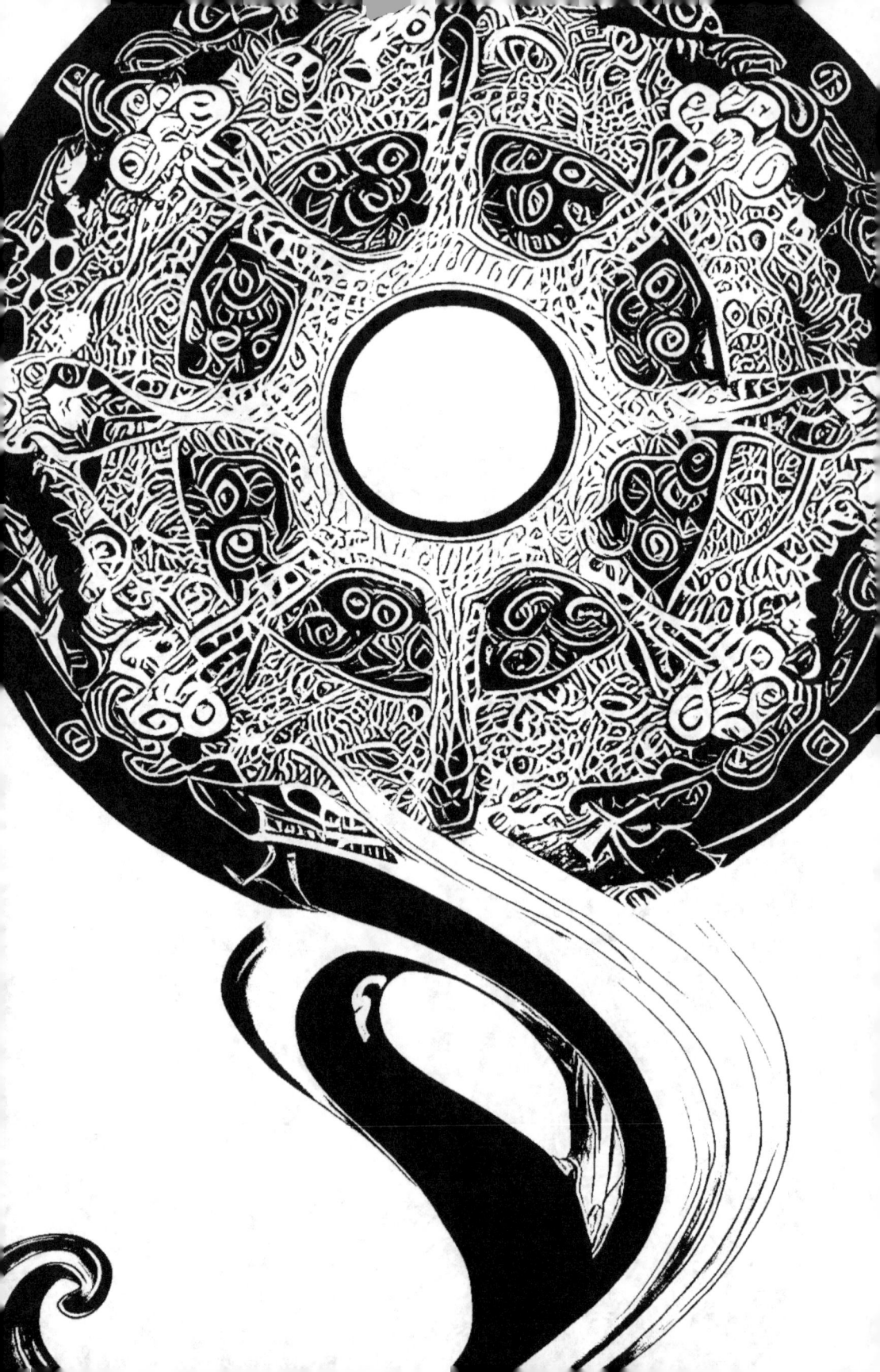

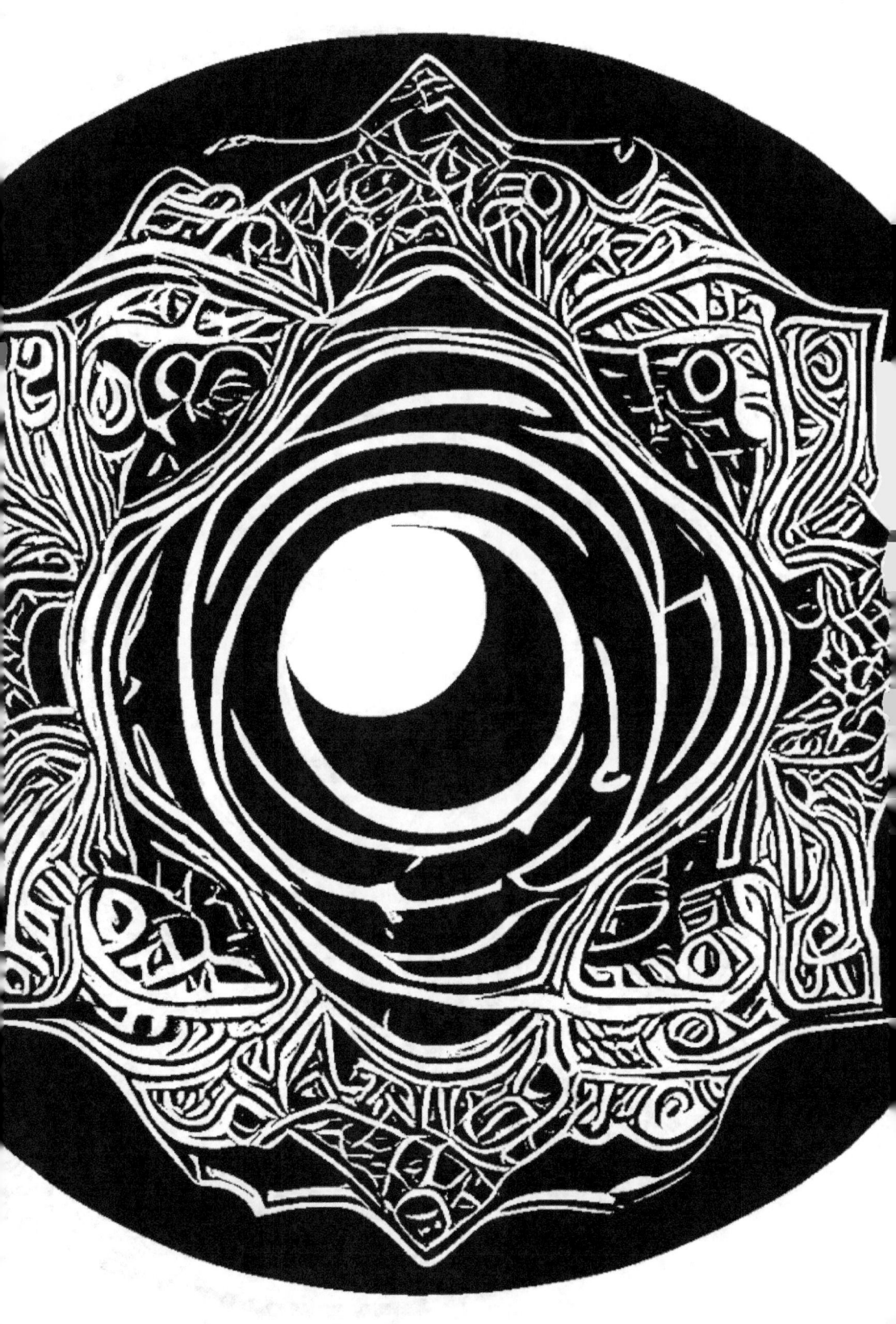

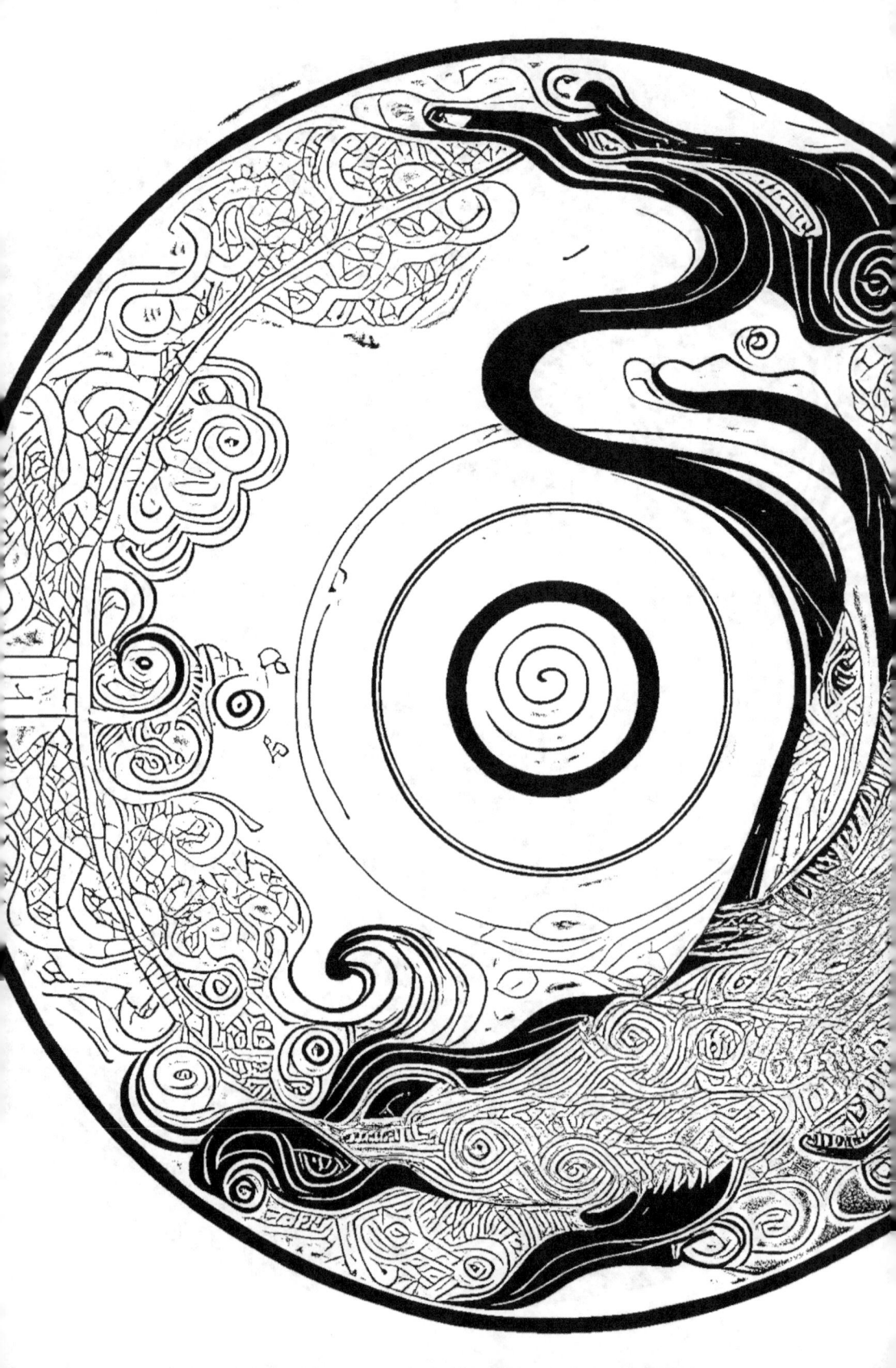

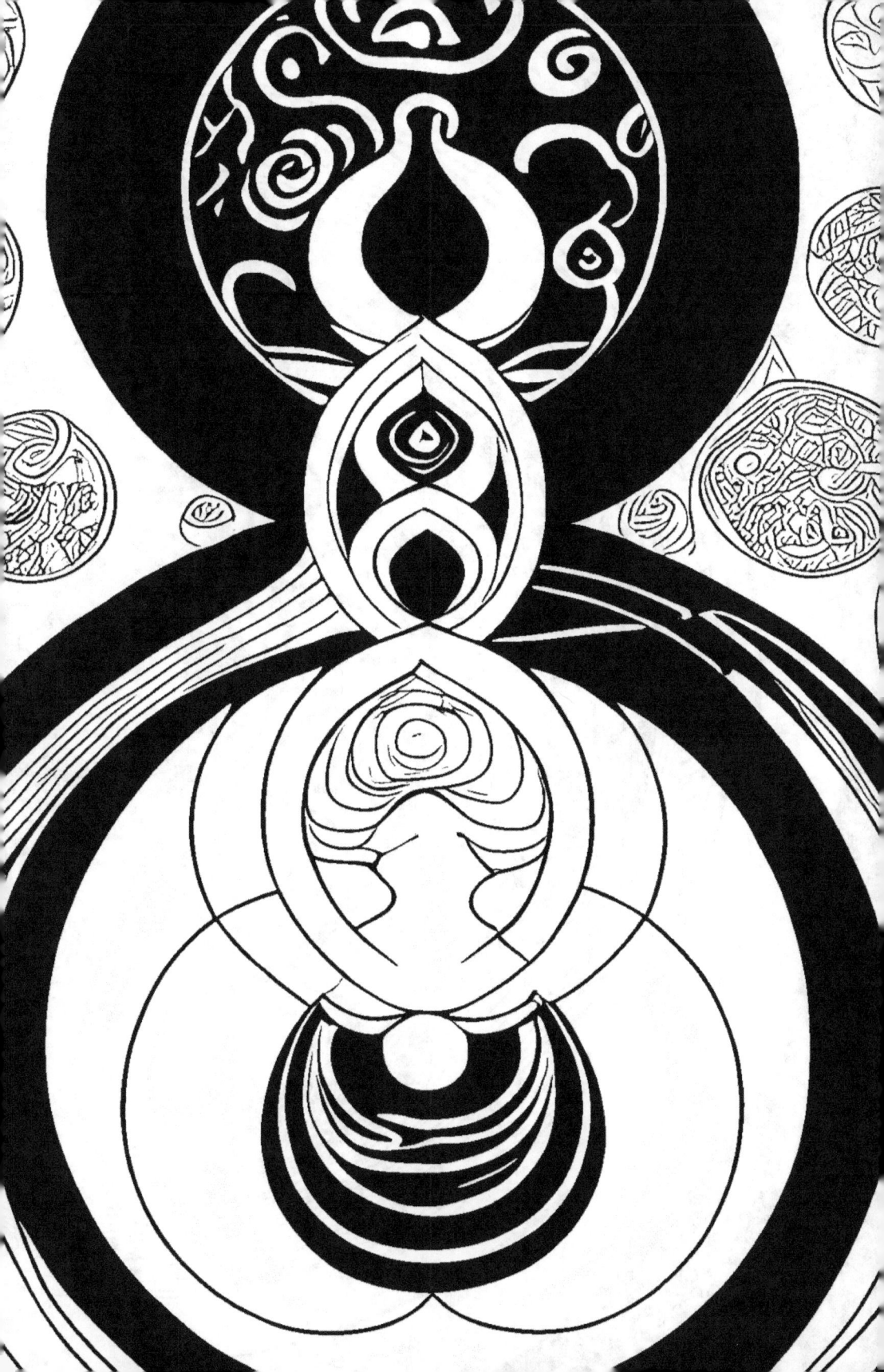

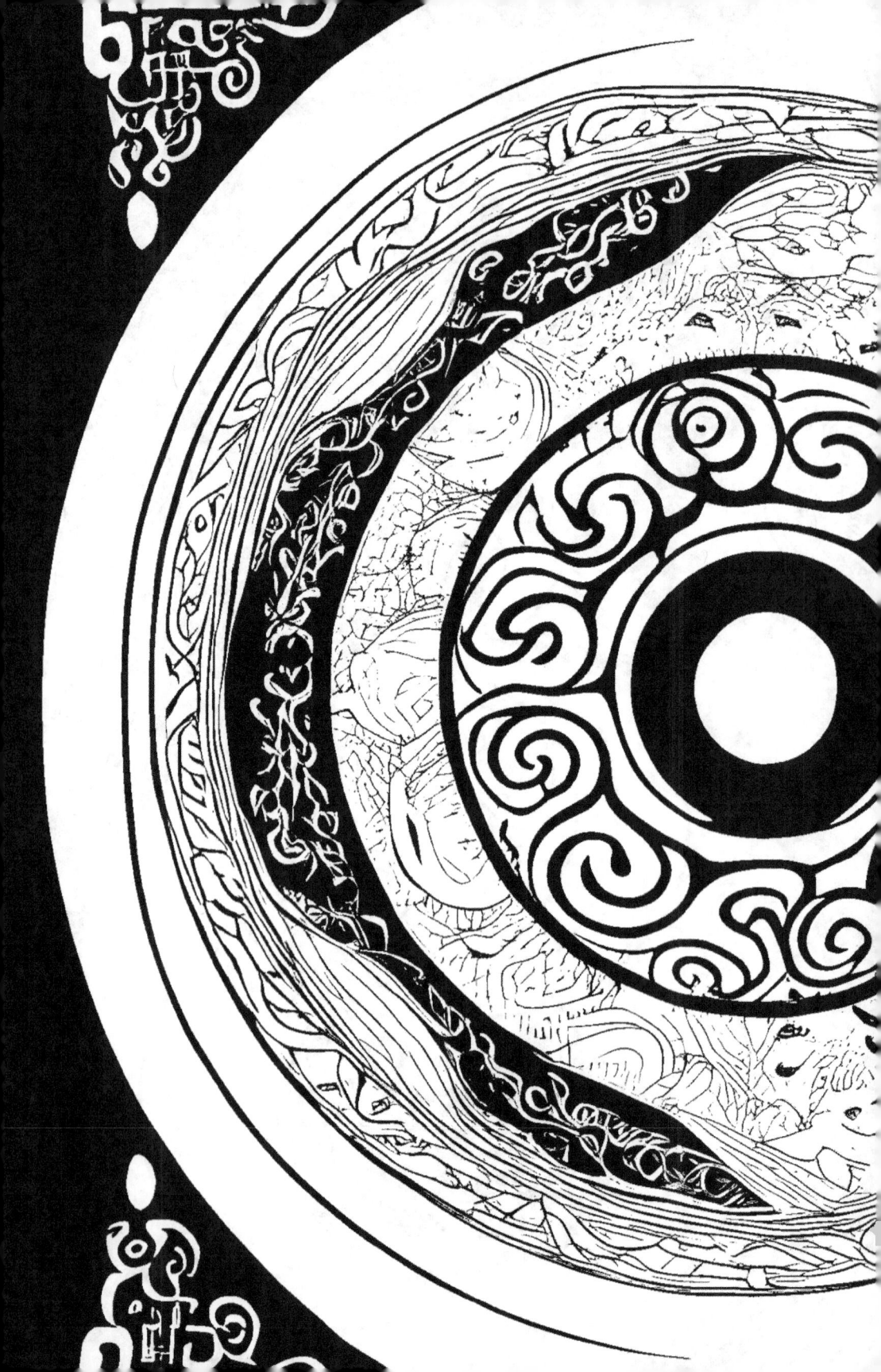

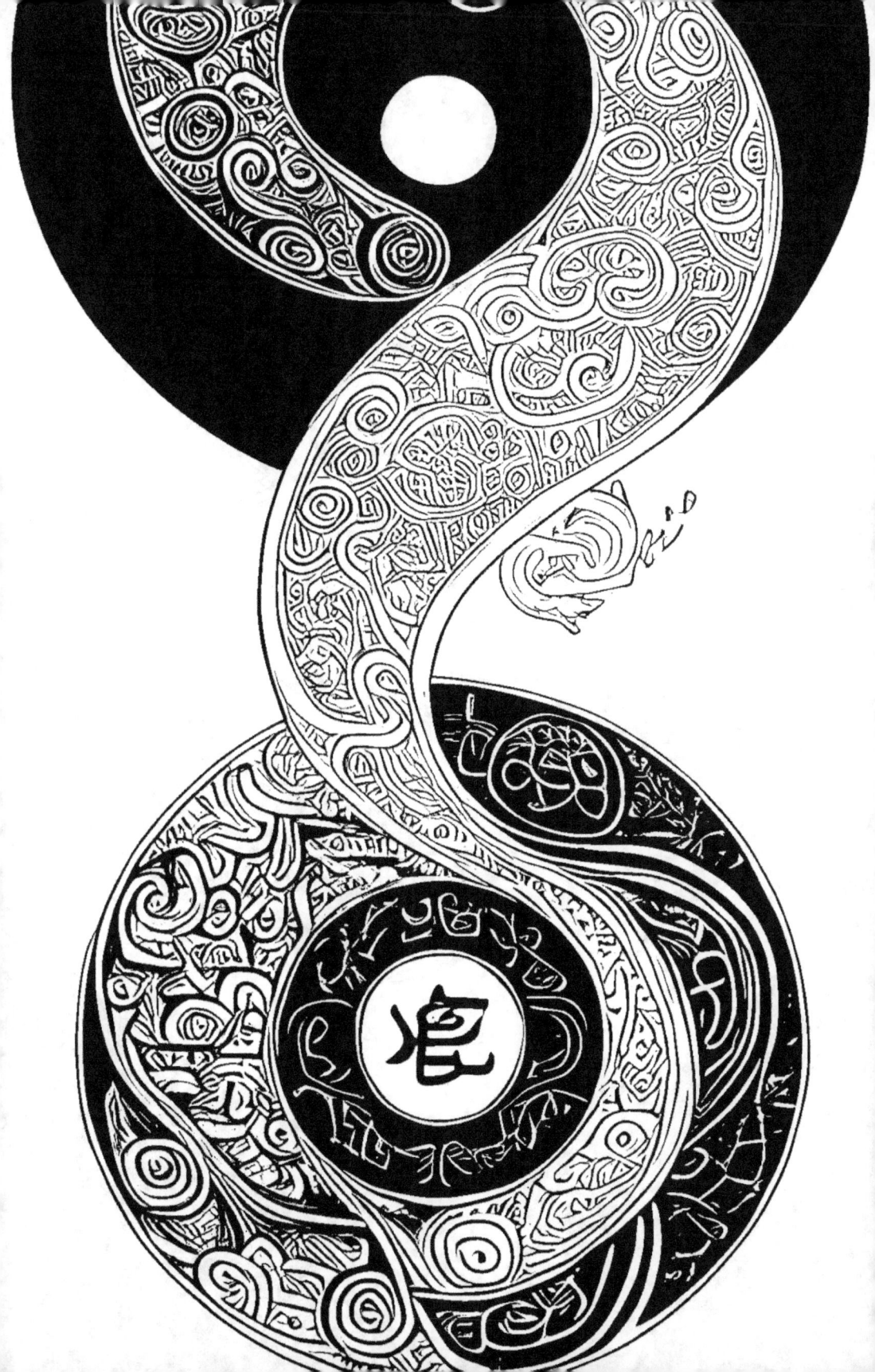

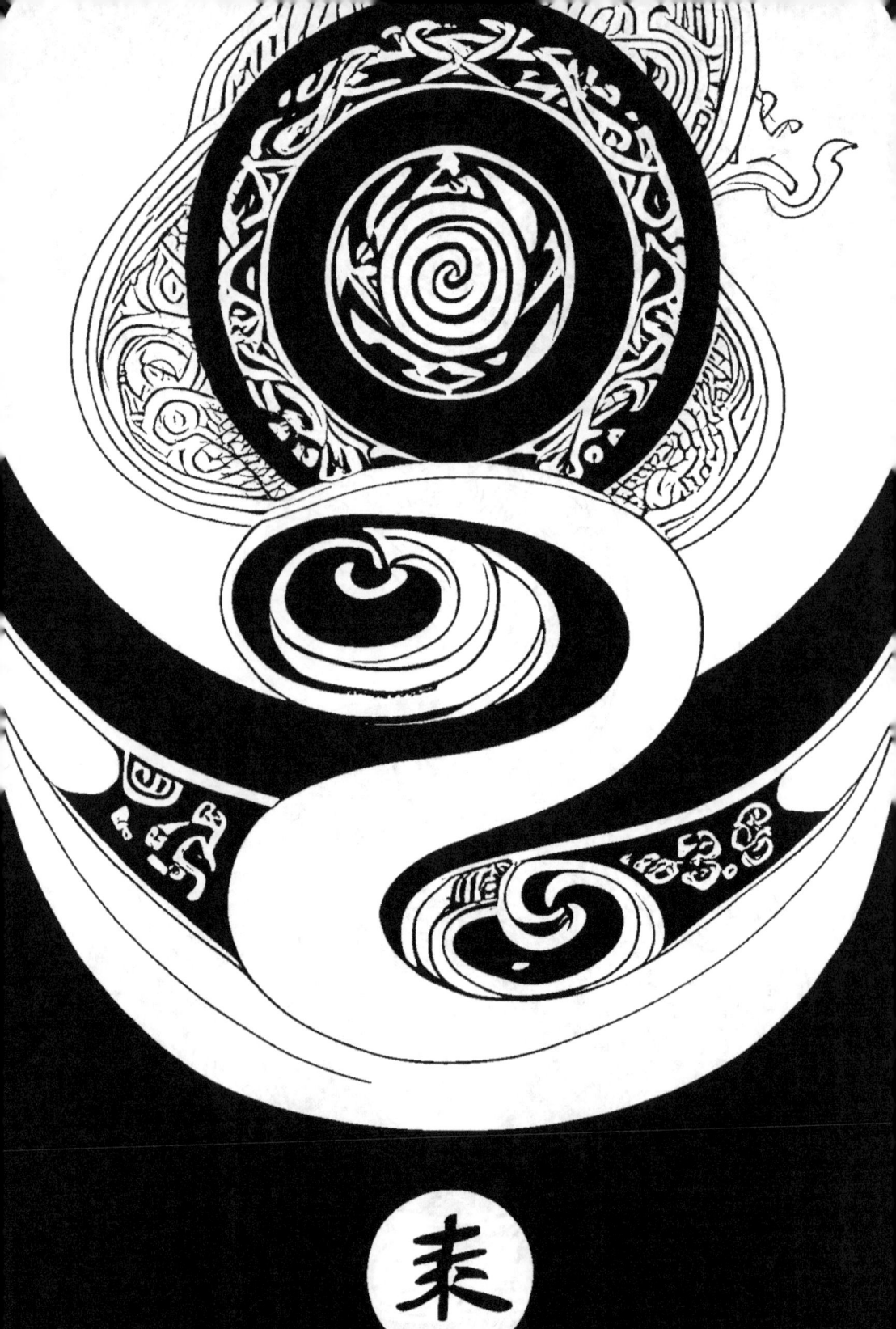

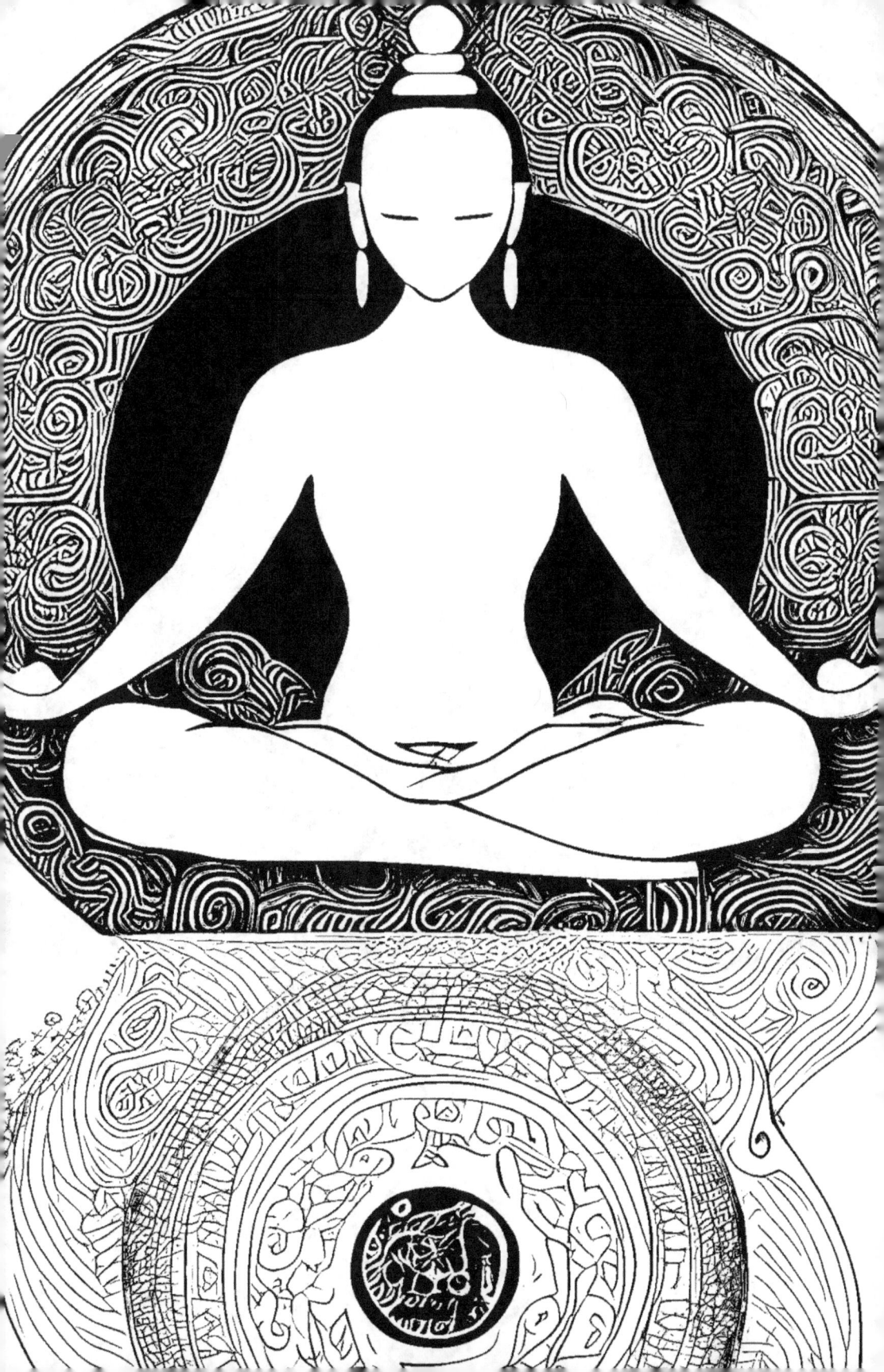

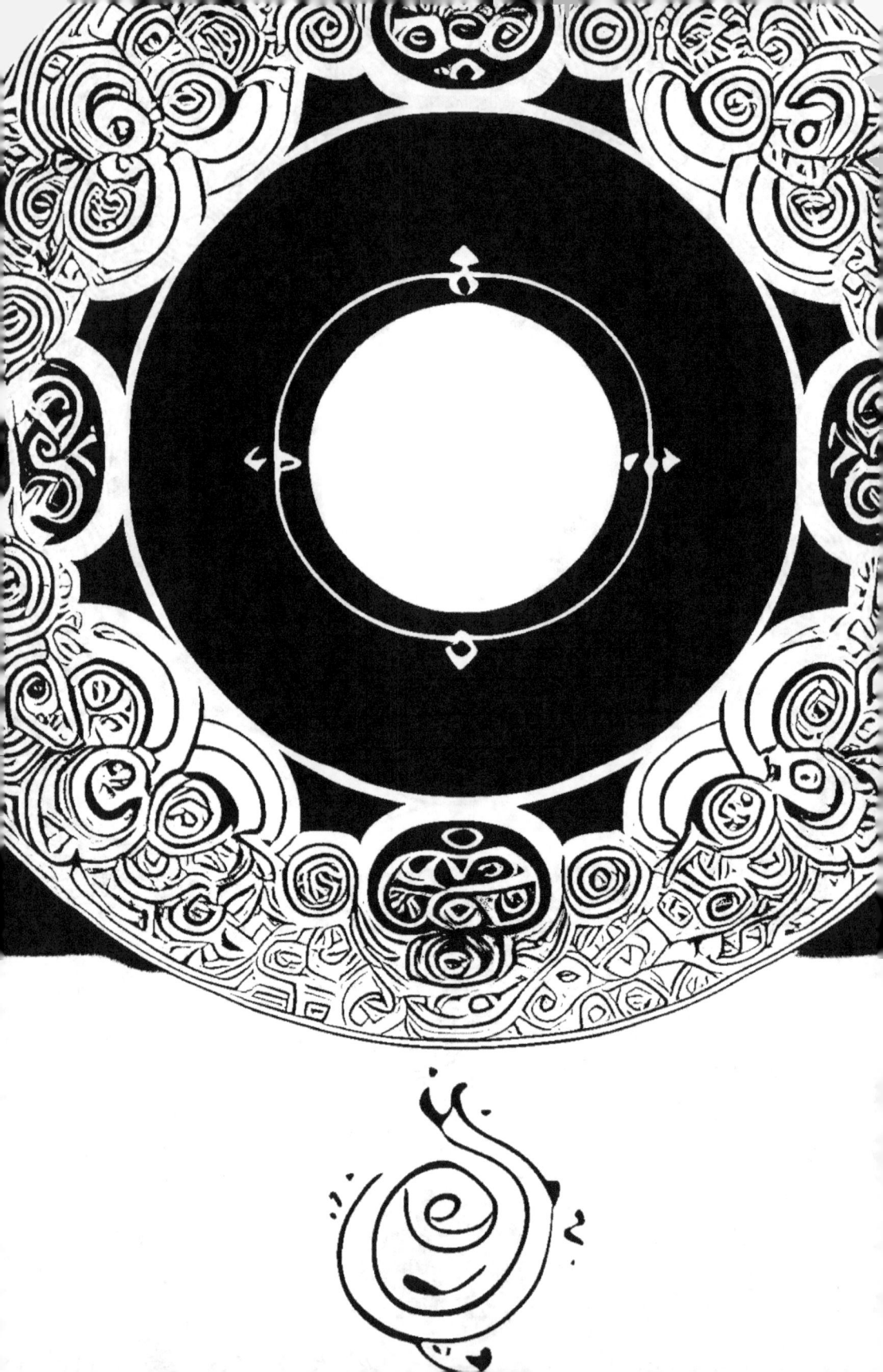

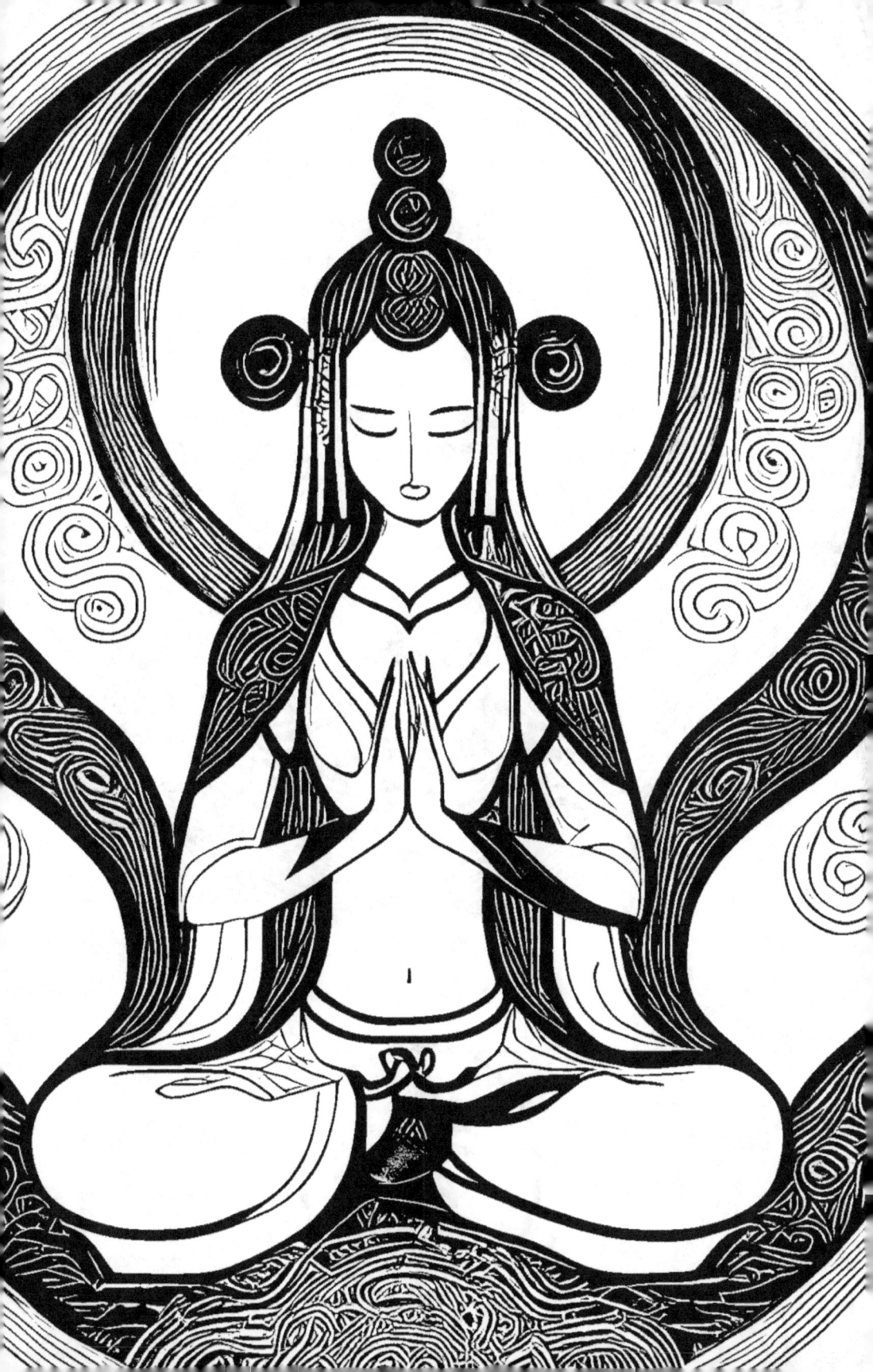

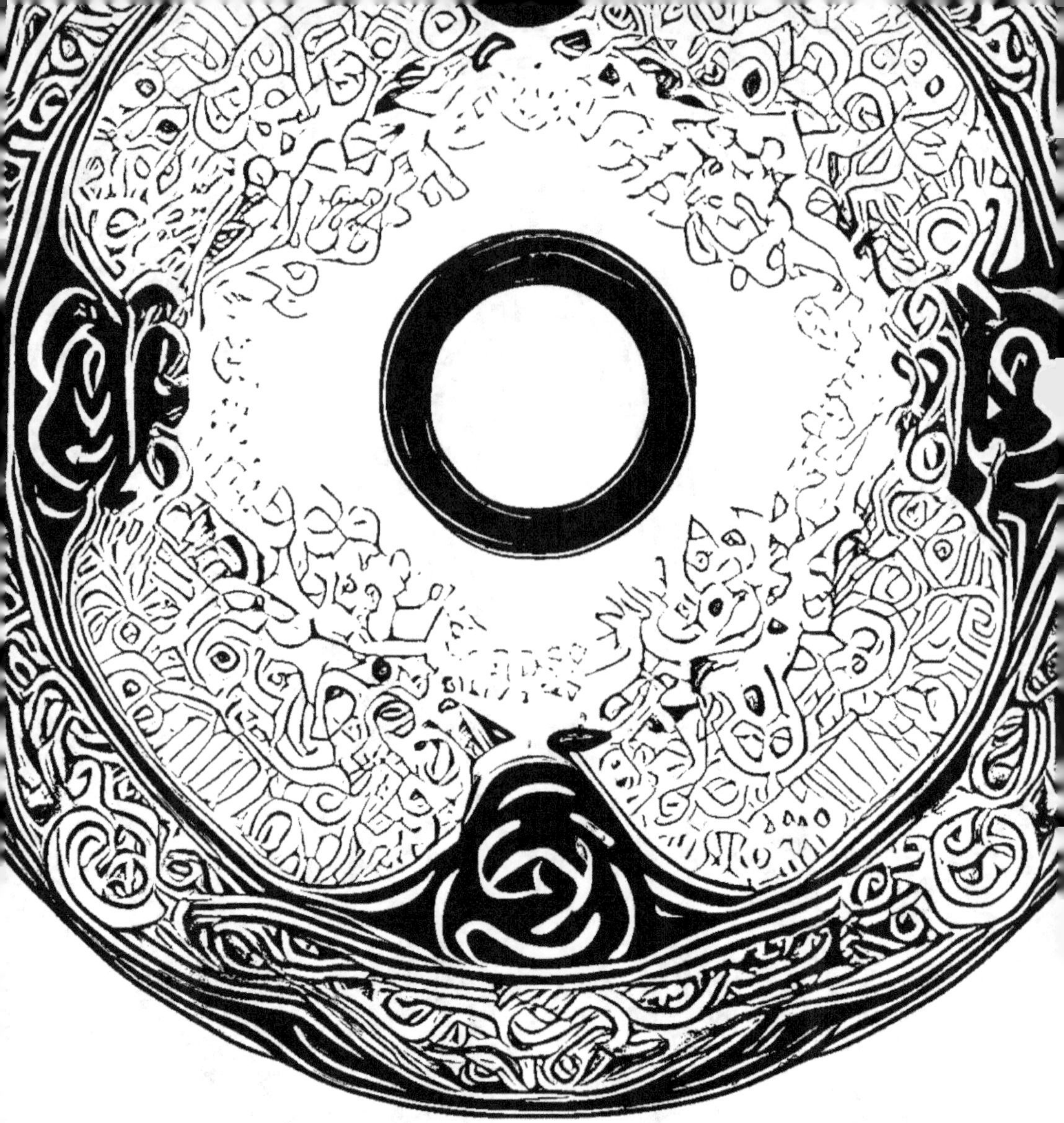

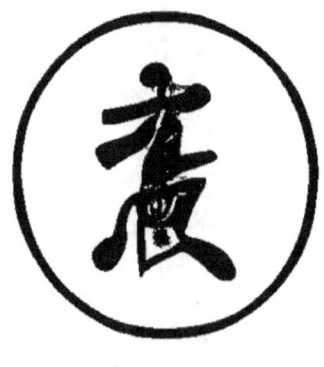

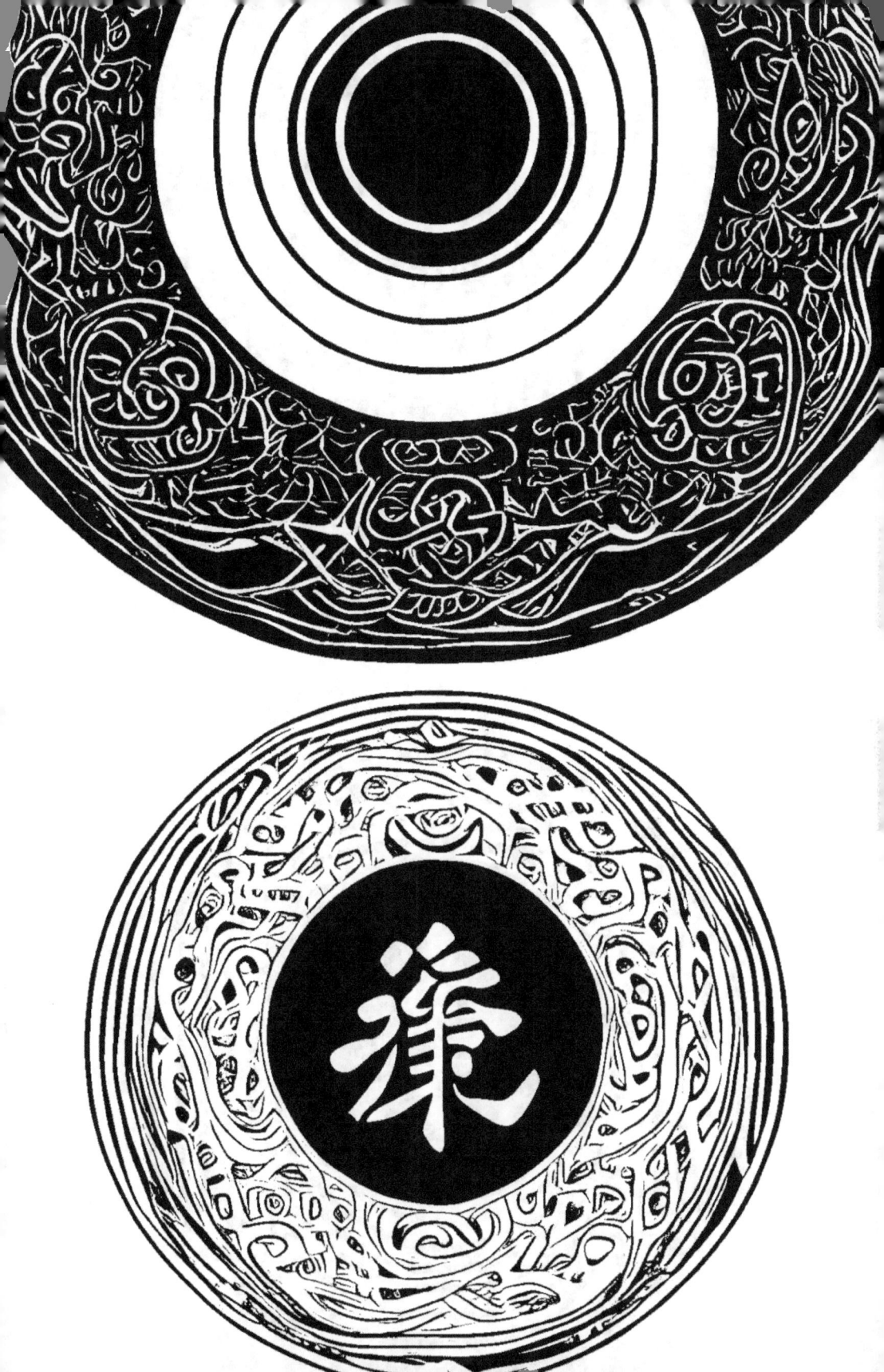

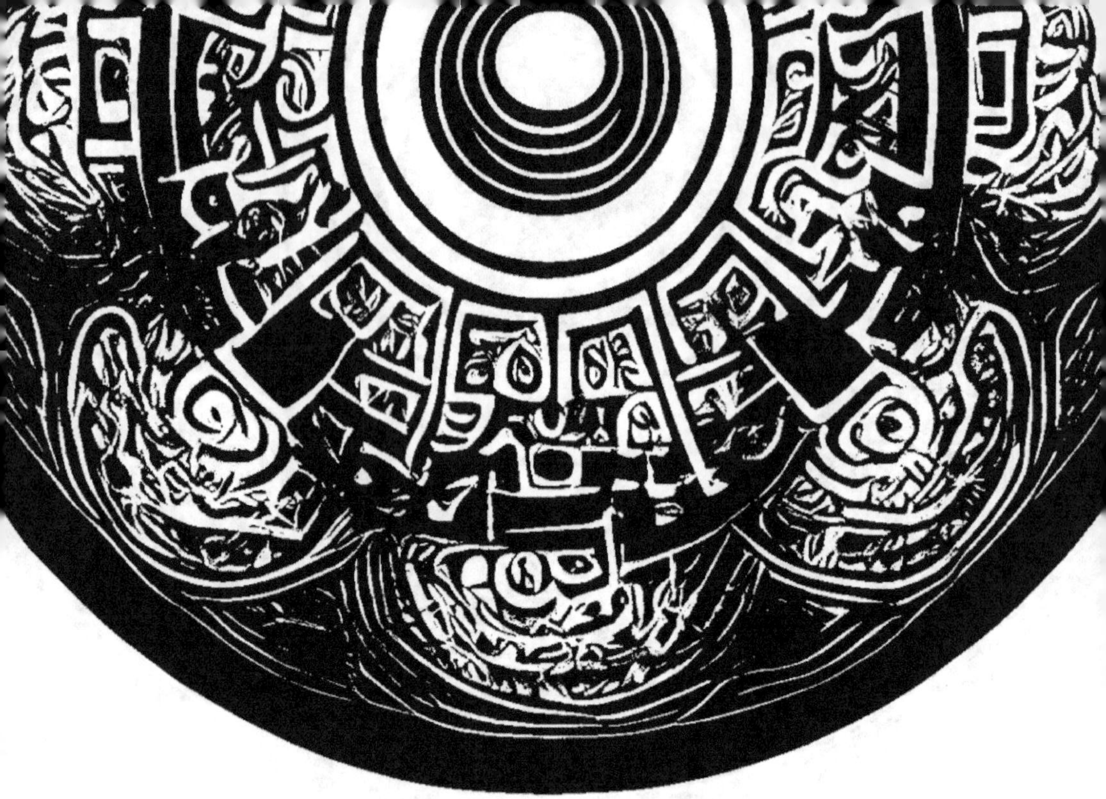

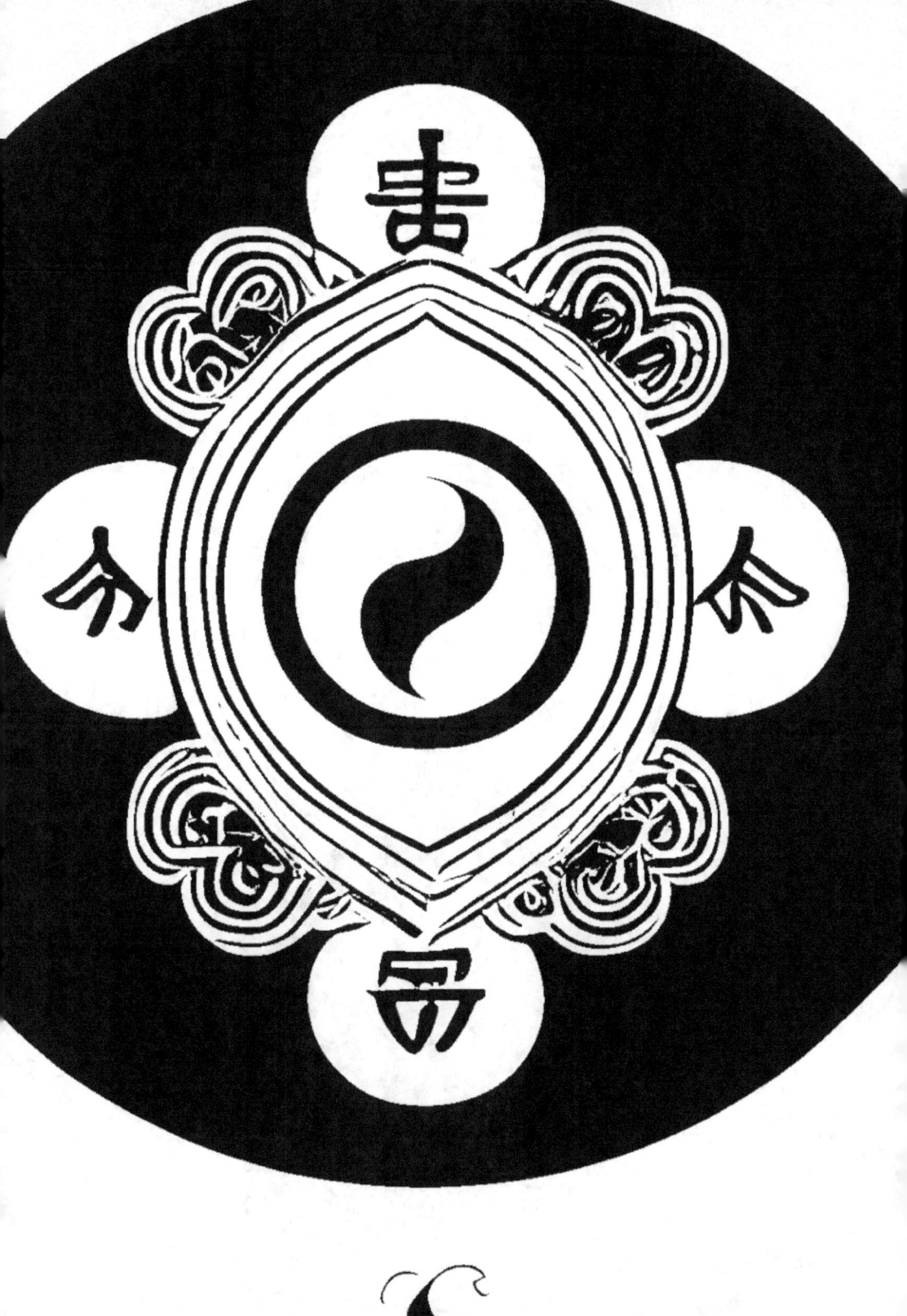

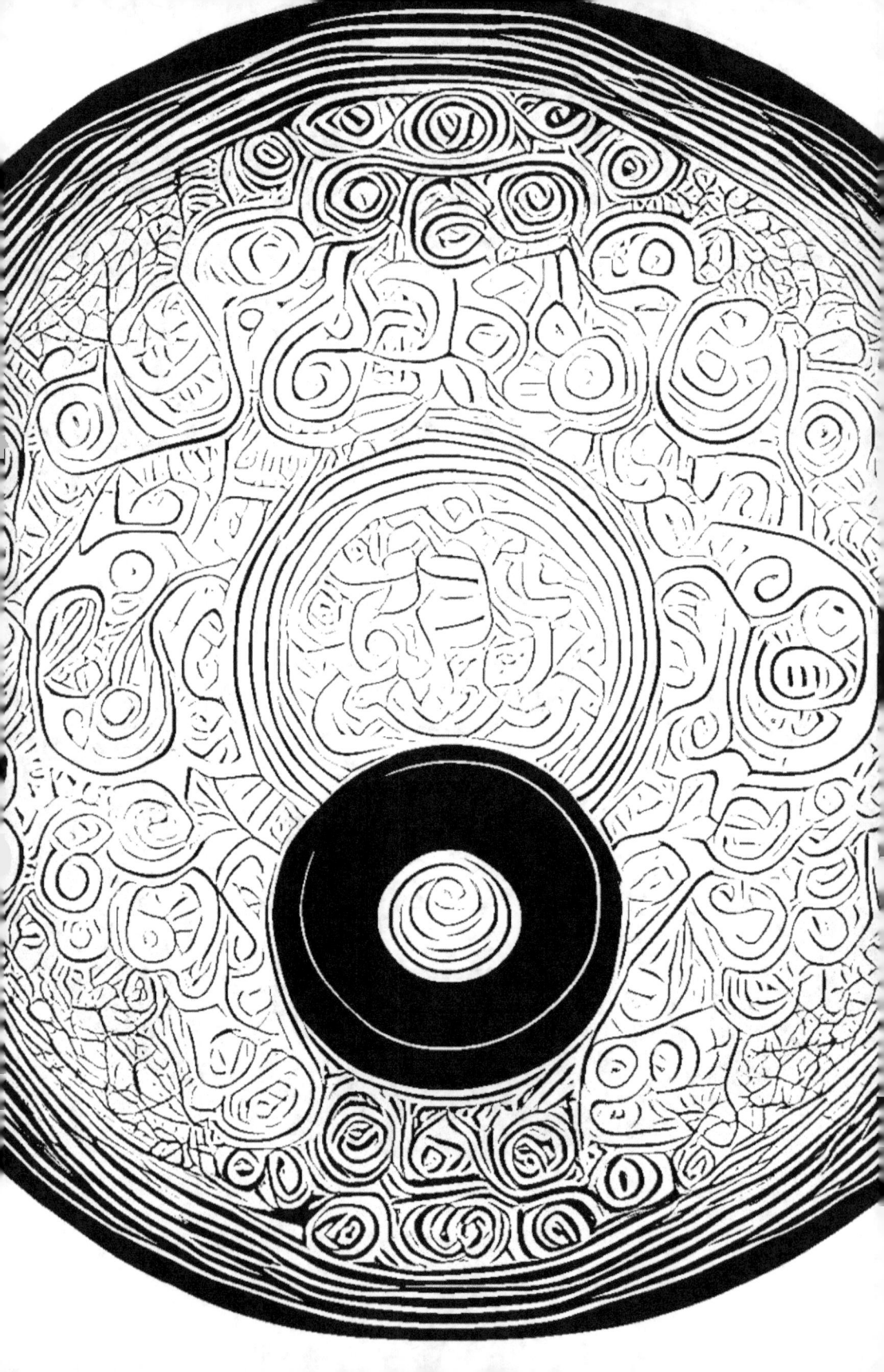

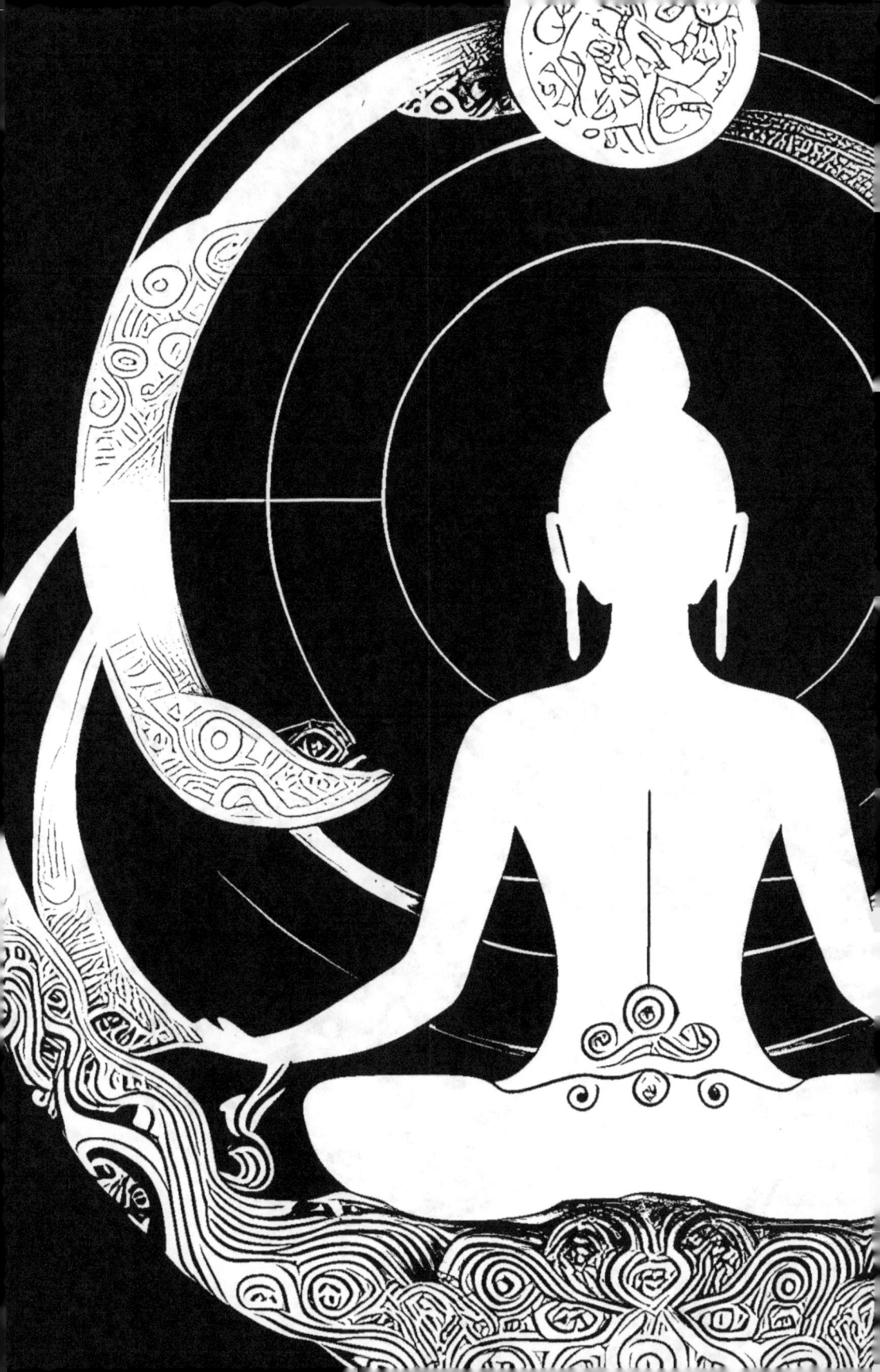

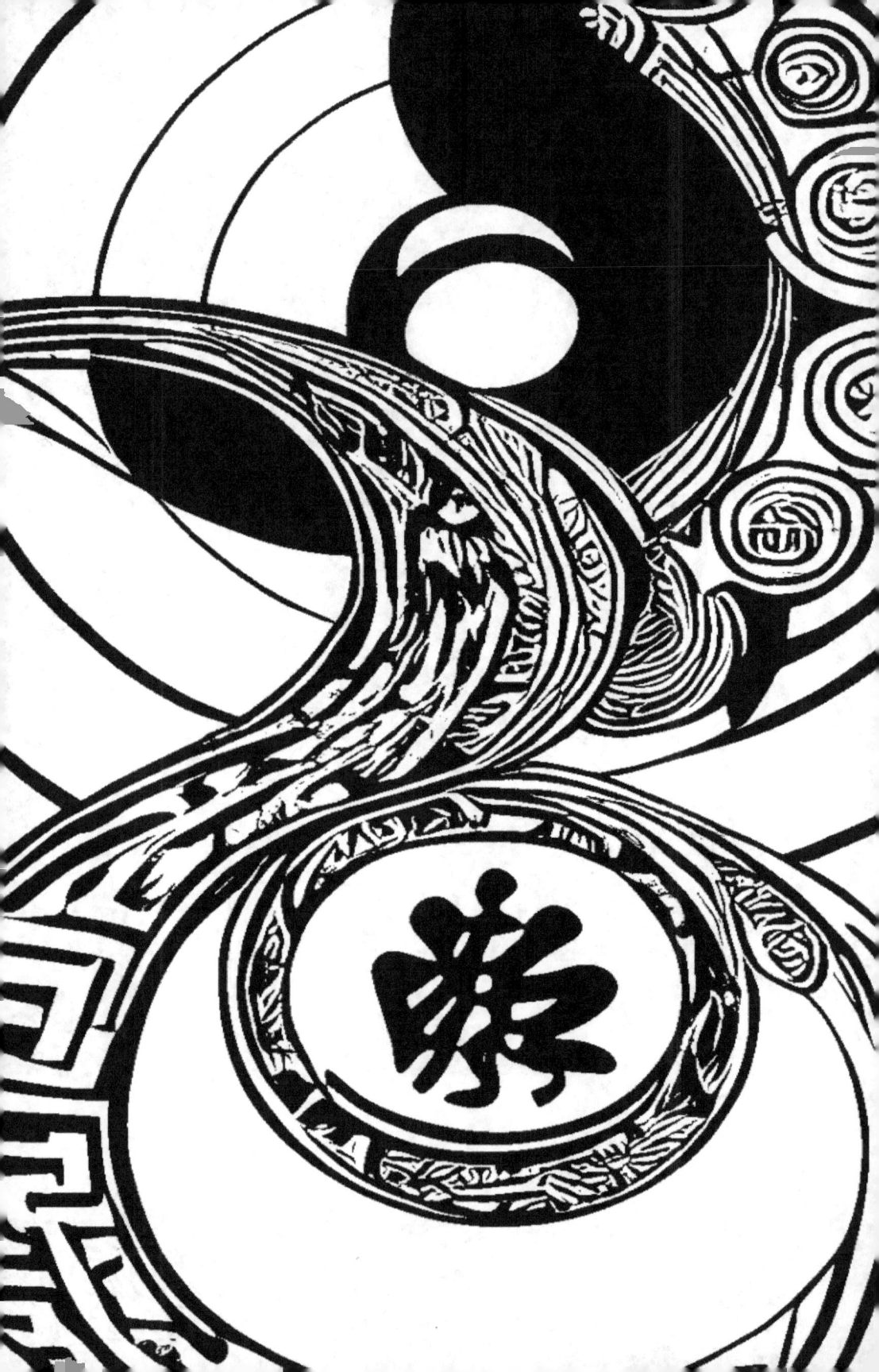

jeremyburt@ishopdailyonline.com jburt_01@hotmail.com
Make Money Online: https://ishopdailyonline.com
Print On Demand: https://ishopdaily.redbubble.com
Print On Demand @ Etsy: https://ishopdailyonline.etsy.com
dj12mind Instrumental Music Albums: https://dj12mind.com
Affiliate Products: https://index.ishopdailyonline.com
Patreon: https://www.patreon.com/user?u=80194438
Facebook: https://www.facebook.com/jeremy.burt2
Youtube:
https://www.youtube.com/channel/UCwV3nApPDh3dNHUGIX4w5nA
tiktok: https://www.tiktok.com/@jeremyburt4?lang=en
amazon: https://www.amazon.com/author/jeremyburt
THANK YOU FOR CHECKING IT OUT!

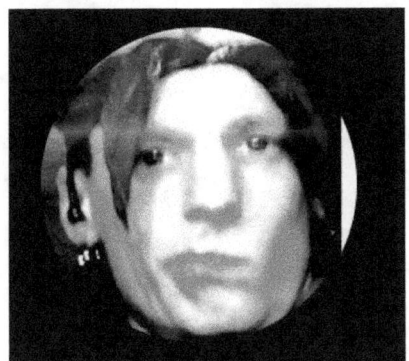

www.ingramcontent.com/pod-product-compliance
Lightning Source LLC
Chambersburg PA
CBHW072239230526
45466CB00025B/2170